THE OAKWOOD PRESS

A Survey of
SEASIDE MINIATURE RAILWAYS

by
D.J. Croft

MINIATURE RAILWAY
Trains leading to -
LEISURE PARK
GARDEN STADIUM
HUMBERSTON FITTIES CAMP
BEACHOLME HOLIDAY CAMP
TRAINS EVERY 15 mins. (approx).

THE OAKWOOD PRESS

© Oakwood Press 1992

ISBN 0 85361 418 0

Typeset by Gem Publishing Company, Brightwell, Wallingford, Oxfordshire.

Printed by Alpha Print (Oxon) Ltd, Witney, Oxfordshire.

The miniature railway at Cleethorpes seen here on 1st June, 1991 showing the new station building at the town-end terminus. *J. Edgington*

Published by
The OAKWOOD PRESS
P.O.Box 122, Headington, Oxford.

Contents

Index of Resorts

Ingoldmells	25	Ramsgate	45
Inverness	130	Ravenglass	120
Isle of Man	126	Rhyl	97
		Romney, Hythe & Dymchurch	45
Jaywick Sands	38	Rochester	41
Jersey	69		
		St Andrews	132
Kessingland	33	St Leonards	53
Kingsbridge	74	Saltburn	10
		Saltwood	45
Littlehampton	57	Sandown	61
Liverpool	104	Saundersfoot	85
Llandudno	95	Scarborough	12
Llanelli	83	Seaburn	10
Lowestoft	32	Seaton Carew	10
Lytham St Annes	109	Severn Beach	80
		Silloth	126
Mablethorpe	23	Skegness	25
Maldon	38	South Shields	9
Margate	41	Southend	38
Maryport	126	Southport	108
Minehead	78	Southsea	60
Morecambe	117	Stokes Bay	63
New Brighton	103	Teignmouth	72
Newquay	75		
		Wells-next-the-Sea	29
Paignton	72	Weston-Super-Mare	80
Penmaenmawr	95	Weymouth	65
Poole	65	Whitby	12
Port Erroll	130	Whitley Bay	9
Porthcawl	83	Withernsea	16
Prestatyn	100	Worthing	57
Pwllheli	92		

A view of 'Hythe – World's Smallest Railway' as stated on this 1930s postcard showing locomotive *Hurricane* on the Romney, Hythe and Dymchurch Railway.

R.W. Kidner

Introduction

The miniature railway is undoubtedly the Cinderella of the railway family. Its standard gauge, and indeed narrow gauge, relations receive far more attention from railway enthusiasts, the general public, and from railway historians. It is paid little attention by the staunchest railway devotee who will travel to the far corners of Britain to see a particular locomotive, railway museum, or even a derelict railway station. Yet this is a pity, for miniature railways are merely scaled-down versions of their larger brethren, and their locomotives are often superb pieces of engineering operating to standards which would not be out of place on a main line railway. There are, of course, exceptions to this, but even a temperamental locomotive of dubious origin giving rides to kiddies beside a paddling pool can often be worth a closer look.

There are scores of miniature railways in operation in Great Britain, and countless more which are no longer in existence. They are to be found at stately homes, seaside resorts, garden centres, popular tourist attractions, local parks, and in fields often hidden from the public gaze. For me, the seaside miniature railway holds the greatest fascination. Perhaps it is the pleasure of returning to some favourite seaside town, and eagerly awaiting the first glimpse of the sea, and the adjacent miniature railway. It may also be the delight in exploring a seaside resort for the first time to find that there is a miniature railway in operation which you were quite unaware of. To embark on a search for miniature railways is to set out on a voyage of discovery – to find, or not to find, a particular line, to discover new rolling stock, and to enjoy the search for information on returning home from a pleasant seaside holiday.

There are differing interpretations of the term 'miniature railway'. Some maintain that a miniature railway is one operated on track between 6 in. (153 mm) and 14 in. (360 mm). To them, 15 in. (381 mm) gauge lines are in a category of their own, and anything larger is termed 'narrow gauge'. However, for the purposes of this book, the term 'miniature railway' is used to cover lines of up to 21 in. (529 mm), as the lines at such places as Scarborough and Blackpool are true miniature railways despite their larger track gauge.

Perhaps at this point it would be wise to offer some explanation of the coverage of this book. The term 'seaside' is used in its broadest sense to include miniature railways which are not merely on the seafront at resorts, but which also lie in the suburbs. Similarly, miniature lines at less well-known locations which are coastal, and connected with the holiday industry are included.

In the pages which follow, well over 100 seaside miniature railways, past and present are described. In some instances, where a line has operated a great number of locomotives, often for very short periods, it is not possible to provide detailed information on all of these, and in such cases, mention may only be made of those with an interesting history, or those which served for long periods of time. Similarly, it is not possible to describe the rolling stock used unless of an unusual nature. Changes of locomotive livery are not recorded unless a significant permanent change was made.

No mention is made of opening times for any of the railways described, for by their very nature, seaside miniature railways are often subject to climatic conditions, and poor patronage in early June, or a sudden downpour in mid-August may force the operator to pack up and go home earlier than intended.

Likewise, no indication of fares is given, for these are subject to constant change. However, where an unusual ticket system is in operation, this may be mentioned.

Finally, no guarantee is made that every line that has ever operated is recorded within these pages, for it is more than possible that a short-lived line in some quiet resort may have evaded even the keenest enthusiast over the years.

If you know of a seaside miniature railway which is not included in this survey, please contact me, via the publishers, in order that further information can be contained in a future edition.   D.J. Croft
December, 1991

Acknowledgements

No work of compiling a book on such a complicated subject as miniature railways can be done in isolation. My thanks therefore go to the many organisations and individuals who have so kindly offered help with information on obscure lines, and allowed me to use illustrations from their collections. In particular I would like to thank the following organisations:

Avon County Council
Bamforth & Co. Ltd
Clwyd County Libraries
Clwyd County Record Office
Essex County Libraries
Humberside Libraries
Ian Allan Ltd
Kent County Libraries
Lancashire County Libraries
Norfolk County Libraries
North Yorkshire County Council
Metropolitan Borough of Sefton Libraries
Severn Lamb Ltd
Wallasey Reference Library

and fellow miniature railway enthusiasts:

S. Andrew, W.J. Ayto, R. Bullock, S.P. Derek, D.W. Dunkerley, I. Gotheridge, C. Judge, R.W. Kidner, F. Mills, J. Morley, M. Oakley, A. Pay, A. Pratt, D.C. Prout, D.T. Rowe, P. Scott, M.P. Simpson, P.T. Theaker, and R. Williams

and finally my thanks go to the numerous miniature railway operators and engine drivers who have patiently answered my questions, and occasionally given me free rides on their trains!

To you all, a big 'Thank You'.

The 15 in. gauge Saltburn Miniature Railway showing the (now demolished) Halfpenny Bridge on 1st August, 1976.

J. Edgington

Prince Charles with a train passing down the valley at Saltburn. The locomotive is a replica of the famous LNER 'A4' class of streamlined locomotives, and was built by George Barlow.

*Photo Courtesy
I. Gotheridge*

Another view in 1965 of Saltburn Miniature Railway showing the *Prince of Wales* locomotive.

J. Edgington

Miniature Railways of North-East England

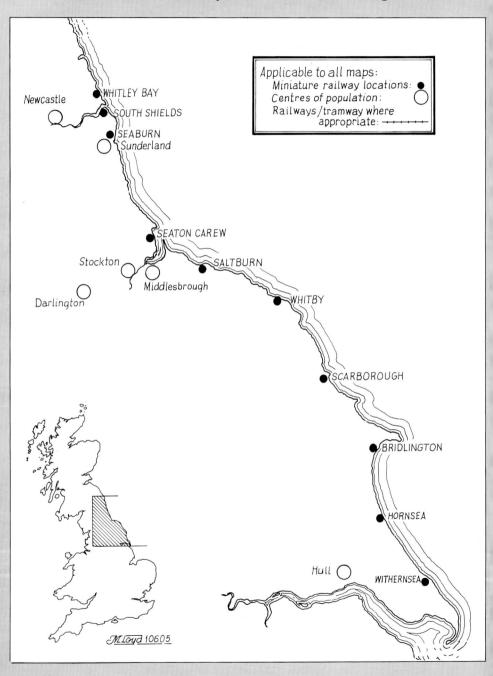

Applicable to all maps:
Miniature railway locations: ●
Centres of population: ○
Railways/tramway where appropriate: +++++++

Newcastle

WHITLEY BAY

SOUTH SHIELDS

SEABURN
Sunderland

SEATON CAREW

Stockton

SALTBURN

Middlesbrough

Darlington

WHITBY

SCARBOROUGH

BRIDLINGTON

HORNSEA

Hull

WITHERNSEA

M.Loyd 10605

Chapter One
North-East England

WHITLEY BAY – GATESHEAD – SOUTH SHIELDS – SEABURN – SEATON
CAREW – SALTBURN – WHITBY – SCARBOROUGH – BRIDLINGTON –
HORNSEA – WITHERNSEA

It is unfortunate that the first seaside resort geographically within north-east England has in fact never had a miniature railway, though it almost did. **Whitley Bay** is popular with day trippers from Newcastle and the surrounding area, and a miniature railway would doubtless have been a great attraction. The local council drew up plans to have a ¼ mile-long line beside the Leisure Pool in 1976, but opposition from local residents caused the plans to be abandoned.

South of the Tyne estuary lies **Gateshead**, venue of the 1990 International Garden Festival. The 200 acre site bordering the river was reclaimed industrial land, and featured a monorail, electric tramcars and a 15 in. gauge miniature railway.

The Festival site was divided into five areas, with the miniature railway linking the Riverside and Dunston areas by means of a girder bridge across the River Team. The railway was designed and built by the Ravenglass & Eskdale Railway and consisted of a single track with a large balloon loop at each end. Trains ran non-stop between the two stations at 'Riverside' and 'Dunston' at approximately 10 minute intervals.

Three locomotives were used on the line, all three being from the Ravenglass & Eskdale Railway:

Northern Rock 2–6–2 built by the Ravenglass & Eskdale Railway in 1976. Yellow livery.
River Irt 0–8–2 built by the Ravenglass & Eskdale Railway in 1928. Green livery.
Shelagh of Eskdale diesel-hydraulic locomotive built by Severn Lamb in 1969. Maroon livery.

River Irt and *Shelagh of Eskdale* worked at the Liverpool Garden Festival in 1984.

Coaching stock consisted of 10 bogie coaches built at Steamtown, Carnforth, comprising seven semi-open vehicles and three saloon brakes. In addition, both the Ravenglass & Eskdale Railway and the Romney, Hythe & Dymchurch Railway provided five saloon coaches each. Carriage stock livery was brown and cream.

Further to the south is the industrial town of **South Shields** which may easily be overlooked as a seaside resort, but it does have long stretches of sandy beach, and many of the attractions of a holiday resort. Close to the sea is South Marine Park which is the home of the Lakeshore Railroad, formerly known as the South Shields Miniature Railway.

The railway is a 9½ in. gauge line, approximately 500 yards in length, running around the edge of the park boating lake. Originally the line was single track throughout, though a passing loop was installed at the station in 1976 to allow two trains to operate simultaneously.

The unusual feature of the Lakeshore Railroad is its locomotive stock. As its name suggests, American style locomotives are used. No. 3440 *Mountaineer* is a 4–6–2 built by Jennings around 1950, whilst its shed-mate is even more interesting. This is an unnamed, unnumbered scale model of a 3 ft gauge 2–6–2 locomotive of the Ferrocarriles Nacionales de Magdalena of Colombia, South America, and is in a distinctive purple livery with green wheels! Rolling stock is more mundane, and consists of a number of open bogie coaches.

At **Seaburn**, on the north side of Sunderland, was the Ocean Park Railroad. This 15 in. gauge line dated back to about 1950, and was operated by the local authority. Originally around ½ mile in length, the track was curtailed to ¼ mile some years ago, and was in the form of a U-shape, trains operating a push-pull service.

The rolling stock of this line included some interesting items. To commence operations, a Herschell Spillman 4–4–0 locomotive was used. This had previously seen service at Southend and Manchester's Belle Vue, and hauled three open bogie carriages which had been on the Blakesley Hall miniature railway. Unfortunately, the locomotive was scrapped, and replaced by a Carland-built 4–6–0 'Royal Scot' locomotive.

Around 1971 the railway was 'dieselised' with the arrival of a four-wheeled petrol locomotive. The railway was in operation in 1980, but appears to have closed shortly afterwards.

Another surprising place at which to find a miniature railway is **Seaton Carew**, a couple of miles south of the port of Hartlepool. For a number of years, a 15 in. gauge line existed here, run by a Mr Dunn who also ran the Whorlton Lido Miniature Railway, near Barnard Castle in Teesdale. No details of rolling stock are known.

Crossing the Tees estuary we come to a trio of small seaside resorts, Redcar, Marske and Saltburn, which have become virtually dormitory towns for the industrial area around Middlesbrough.

When the 15 in. gauge line at **Saltburn** was built in 1948, the town was in the North Riding of Yorkshire. Local Government reorganisation in 1974 changed that, so now the town and its miniature railway are in the County of Cleveland. The line was originally owned by the local bus company, Saltburn Motor Services. They built the single track ¾ mile line from Cat Nab station, near the seafront, inland to the Valley Gardens. The only structure on the line was a bridge over a stream.

The line was initially operated with a 2–4–0 petrol-driven locomotive which had once run at Great Yarmouth. Then in 1950 a most historic locomotive was acquired. This was *Elizabeth*, a 4–4–4 tank engine. Originally built in 1909 by Bassett-Lowke for the Squire of Blakesley's private line in Northamptonshire, it was then named *Blacolvesley*. It was unusual, if not unique, at that time in being powered by a motor car engine, yet retaining a steam locomotive outline. It ran on the Squire's estate until 1943, though its whereabouts from then until 1950 are not clear.

About 1960, another locomotive was acquired. This was *Prince Charles*, which had previously operated on the Lakeside Miniature Railway at Southport. It was based on the famous 'A4' class streamlined Pacific engines

A 1950s view of the North Bay Miniature Railway at Scarborough showing one of the two Hudswell Clarke's 4–6–2 locomotives about to leave Peasholm station with a full load of holidaymakers. *Author's Collection*

A modern view of the North Bay Miniature Railway at Scarborough taken on 24th September, 1989 showing the temporary terminus being used due to sewer works near to the Scalby Mills station. Notice the coaches now have top covers. *John Edgington*

which were working on the East Coast main line, and was one of several built by Harry Barlow. Unfortunately, these locomotives did not have the same successful styling of their larger brothers. *Prince Charles* was soon renamed *Prince of Wales* and proved to be an extremely reliable locomotive. It was in reality a diesel-electric locomotive, for its Fordson tractor engine was coupled to a dynamo.

In 1974 the railway changed hands, for Saltburn Motor Services was bought out by Cleveland Transit. They ran the line for the rest of the 1974 season, but in 1975 the line passed into the ownership of the Langbaurgh Borough Council. Shortly afterwards, the bridge over the stream had to be demolished, and the track at the seaward end was therefore isolated and lifted, thus rendering the line inoperable, for the station and engine shed were situated in this area. *Prince of Wales* was subsequently acquired for preservation.

For several years the line lay derelict, and suffered a great deal of vandalism. In 1980, reconstruction of the railway began by Mr Brian Leonard, and trains ran once again using *Prince of Wales* which was brought out of retirement.

Unfortunately, the line did not reopen in 1982, but the following year the Saltburn Miniature Railway Association was formed to restore and operate the line. In 1985 the Langbaurgh Borough Council gave permission for work to begin, and on 29th August, 1987, the line finally reopened, having been completely rebuilt and the rolling stock overhauled.

Whitby was the location of the next miniature railway down the coast from Saltburn. Here on the north side of the River Esk was the West Cliff Miniature Railway. A 10¼ in. gauge line was built in 1969, and was at one time run by the Ian Allan Organisation, and the line's earliest locomotive was a Shepperton-built diesel named *Meteor II*. The railway was 300 yards long in the form of an irregular circle.

In the early 1980s a Severn Lamb 'Rio Grande' steam-outline diesel locomotive in maroon livery was in use, together with five open articulated bogie coaches. During this time the railway was marketed as 'Tuby's Train'. It is believed to have last operated in the summer of 1985.

Apart from the Ravenglass & Eskdale and Romney, Hythe & Dymchurch miniature railways, perhaps the best known seaside miniature line is the North Bay Railway at **Scarborough**. The line's greatest asset is the fact that it is an end-to-end line about ⅔ mile long, in place of the more usual loop of track.

Plans for the resort's miniature railway took shape in 1930, when a 15 in. gauge line was first suggested. The site for the line was an area of land known locally as 'Hodgson's Slack', close to the north bay which was being developed as a pleasure park. By the time construction work began in January 1931, the gauge had been changed to 20 in. The work was completed in record time, and the line was opened on Whit Saturday, 23rd May, 1931 by the Mayor of Scarborough.

The station at the southern end of the line is named 'Peasholm', after the nearby park of that name. Behind the station, and well-hidden by the trees is

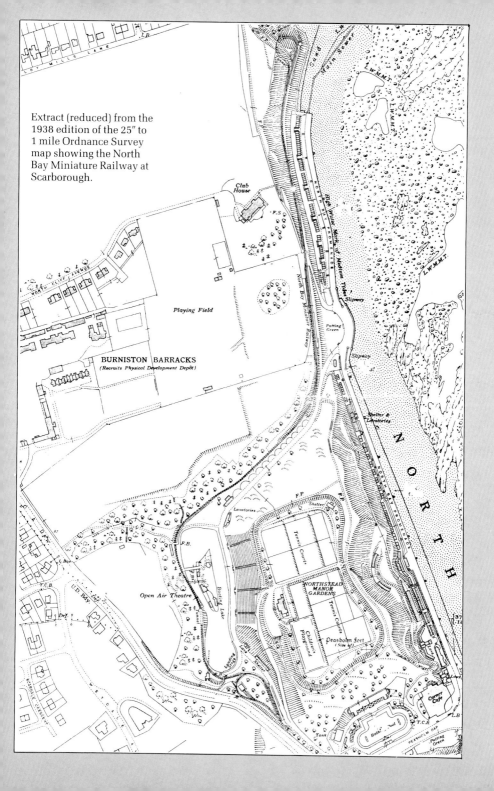

Extract (reduced) from the 1938 edition of the 25″ to 1 mile Ordnance Survey map showing the North Bay Miniature Railway at Scarborough.

the engine shed, which can be reached from either end of the station plat-form by means of a triangular loop line.

On leaving the station, the line soon passed beneath the water chute, and traversed one side of the boating lake, partly in tunnel. At the end of the lake, the line passed through the shrubbery for quite some distance before reaching the sea at Beach station. From here, the line ran parallel to the sea behind a lengthy row of beach huts, before reaching the station at Scalby Mills. Here, a turning loop partly in tunnel enabled the engine to turn round its train before returning to Peasholm.

After the first season of operation, the track layout at Peasholm was altered to provide a stock siding at the station, and a run-round loop via the locomotive shed to reach the front of the train. At the same time the layout of the intermediate Beach station was altered, so that two trains could be operated. The track was doubled at Beach, and an additional platform built, though the station itself was never used by passengers, being used merely as a halt to enable the other train to pass by in the opposite direction.

The railway managed to keep open in the early part of the war, but closed in July 1940, and all nameboards were removed the following month. Easter 1945 saw the reopening of the line, and at times it was necessary to remove bits from one engine to keep the other in service. As conditions eased, it was possible to relay the entire track in 1947. For the next 15 years the line ran with little alteration, but the next two decades were to see dramatic changes at Scalby Mills.

In the early 1960s a major redevelopment scheme was announced for the whole of the Scalby Mills area, and amongst the first changes was the removal of the tunnel in 1962. A new entertainment complex was built close to the railway. In 1977 a new station was built at Scalby Mills, which included a covered platform, and a revised track layout.

From the start of the 1988 season the line has been subject to major disruption, as the Yorkshire Water Authority began constructing a new sewage pumping station at Scalby Mills, which necessitated the closure of the area. As a result, trains temporarily ran only as far as Beach station, which had not previously seen passenger use. The work is expected to take until the spring of 1991 to complete, after which the railway will be restored to Scalby Mills. The consequent shortening of the line means that only one train is in use at a time, and as no turning facilities exist at Beach station, trains are propelled backwards to Peasholm station.

The one feature of the North Bay Railway which has remained constant over the years is the rolling stock. For the opening, a Hudswell Clarke 4–6–2 steam-outline diesel locomotive (Works No. D565) was delivered. This was numbered 1931, and named *Neptune*. As traffic increased, a second identical locomotive (Works No. D573) was obtained in 1932, and appropriately numbered 1932, and named *Triton*. Both locomotives are replicas of LNER 'Pacifics', and are in green livery, and are still in regular use today. Other details of the locomotives are:

Driving wheels: 28 in. diameter; Overall length: 26 ft 1 in.; Weight: 10¼ tons; Maximum height: 5 ft 5 in.; Maximum Width: 4 ft 0 in.; Westinghouse air brakes, plus hand brakes.

A commercial postcard view of Northstead Manor Gardens, Scarborough with the miniature railway on the extreme left. On the right of the lake is the vast open-air theatre seating 7,000 people.
Oakwood Collection

A full loaded five-coach passenger train on the North Bay Miniature Railway at Scarborough.
Author's Collection

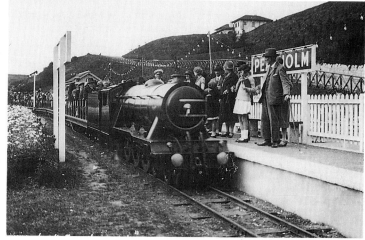

'Just arrived at Scarborough' reads the postcard. Again a fully loaded passenger train on the North Bay railway at Peasholm station, Scarborough.
Author's Collection

Over the years there have been plans for new locomotives, though none have ever materialised.

Rolling stock consists of 10 open toast-rack bogie coaches, each seating 20 passengers. In recent years, a number have been fitted with canvas top covers to provide shelter for passengers.

Surprisingly, **Bridlington**, 16 miles down the coast from Scarborough does not have a miniature railway among its current attractions. In the early 1950s the local council drew up plans for a miniature line to run from the north-east outskirts of the town to Sewerby Park. However, opposition from local residents meant that the line was never built.

A miniature railway was, however, built in the resort at about the same time, for in 1951 a 7¼ in. gauge line was moved to the resort from Llandudno. This was situated on the South Promenade close to the Spa. The single track ran parallel to the promenade for a short distance after leaving the station, and then turned inland running along the side of the boating lake. A right turn along the lake brought the line to its other station near the Spa. A run-round loop existed at both ends, and the track is believed to have been between 100 yards and 160 yards long. Until 1965 two steam locomotives were used. These were a model of a Southern Railway 4−4−0, and an 0−6−0 saddle tank. After 1965 two diesel locomotives were used, these being a 'Deltic', and an 0−6−0 shunter which had been built by the operator. The railway was still in use in 1967, but had gone by 1971.

Some 15 miles south of Bridlington lies the small resort of **Hornsea**. Although this quiet seaside town does not have a miniature railway nowadays, two are known to have existed in the past.

The earliest line appeared in the early 1930s, being of 10¼ in. gauge and situated on the seafront. Little else is known of this line, except that it featured a wooden station which was reached by means of a footbridge. Motive power consisted of a Bassett-Lowke North Eastern Railway 4−4−2 locomotive and three 4-seater coaches with glass end-screens from the same builder. It is believed that the railway was run by a company which also had lines at Cleethorpes, Cleveleys and Saltburn. At the same time, the local council was opposed to the railway operating on Sundays, and so eventually the line was dismantled and moved. There is evidence to suggest that the locomotive later appeared on the company's line at Saltburn, and still later at the other end of the country at Severn Beach where it was noted in 1936.

The second Hornsea line was in existence in 1936, and is thought to have been of 7¼ in. gauge. It too was situated close to the seafront, and ran round a model boating lake. The locomotive used was a model of a Great Central Railway 4−4−2 which had been subsequently rebuilt, and was lettered LNER 1933 on the tender. No further details are known of this line.

Our final visit in North-East England is to **Withernsea**, sixteen miles south of Hornsea. Here, a 9½ in. gauge line was established in 1934 close to the Floral Hall. The ¼-mile long circuit of track enclosed the Hall and a boating lake, and much of the line was in a cutting. The only motive power was an 'Atlantic' 4−4−2 locomotive named *Lily*, built by Parver Models of Southport. The fate of the line is not known, and the resort does not have a miniature railway at present.

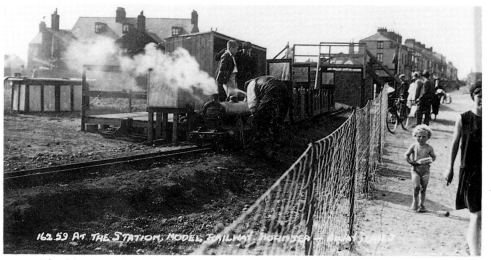

The driver attends to his engine in this 1930s view of the short 10¼ in. gauge line at Hornsea. The locomotive is a Bassett-Lowke 4–4–2. The small child to the right of the picture seems unimpressed by the display of smoke from the locomotive.

Courtesy I. Gotheridge

'Tuby's Train' on the miniature railway at Whitby seen here in the early 1980s. The Severn Lamb-constructed locomotive *Rio Grande* was at this time painted in maroon livery. Unfortunately this railway closed in 1985.

Oakwood Collection

Miniature Railways of Eastern England

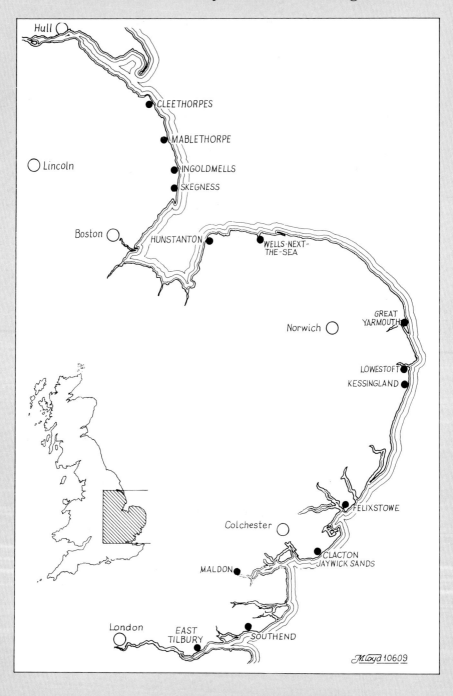

Hull ◯

● CLEETHORPES

● MABLETHORPE

◯ Lincoln

● INGOLDMELLS

● SKEGNESS

Boston ◯

HUNSTANTON ●

● WELLS·NEXT-
THE-SEA

Norwich ◯

GREAT
YARMOUTH ●

LOWESTOFT ●

KESSINGLAND ●

Colchester ◯

● FELIXSTOWE

● CLACTON
JAYWICK SANDS

MALDON ●

London ◯

EAST
TILBURY

● SOUTHEND

M.Loyd 10609

Chapter Two
Eastern England

CLEETHORPES – MABLETHORPE – INGOLDMELLS – SKEGNESS –
HUNSTANTON – WELLS – GREAT YARMOUTH – LOWESTOFT –
KESSINGLAND – FELIXSTOWE – CLACTON – JAYWICK – MALDON –
SOUTHEND – EAST TILBURY

Crossing the estuary of the River Humber, the first resort we come to is
Cleethorpes, where the miniature railway celebrated its 40th birthday in
1988, though it has changed considerably since it was first built.
The first line was constructed in 1948 to a gauge of 10¼ in., and was
approximately a ½ mile in length, running parallel to the boating lake on the
Marine Embankment at the south end of the seafront. Motive power consisted of *Cleethorpes Flyer*, a one-fifth scale model of the LNER locomotive
Flying Scotsman.
In 1954 the line changed hands, being purchased by a Mr Arthur Clethro
of Scarborough. Under his ownership the line was changed to accumulator
traction with battery-charging units at each of the two stations which were
named 'Cleethorpes' and 'Thrunscoe'. To operate the line, three battery-
powered 4–6–4 locomotives were acquired, though in service they ran with
the driving wheels disconnected. No further details are known of these
engines.
A number of the open bogie coaches used on this line were subsequently
used on the Olicana Miniature Railway at Ilkley, in West Yorkshire.
Another change of ownership came in 1959 when the line was purchased
by Cleethorpes Borough Council who operated it basically as it was until
1972.
In that year the line was entirely rebuilt, extended and regauged. The
previous terminal station at Thrunscoe became an intermediate halt, and the
line was extended southwards to the zoo, making it four-fifths of a mile in
length. The new gauge adopted was an unusual 14½ in. To operate the re-
equipped line, the second of the Severn Lamb 'Rio Grande' 2–8–0 locomotives (Works No. 7217) was built specially for the line. The locomotive,
which was unnumbered, was unusual in that it had a propane gas con-
version unit fitted to its engine. Also new was another model of the *Flying
Scotsman*, built by R&A Developments of Scunthorpe.
In 1978 a second 'Rio Grande' locomotive was purchased (Works
No. 15–7–78), this one having an ornamental balloon stack chimney, and a
large square headlamp. Livery was maroon, and the locomotive was
numbered 800. This locomotive replaced the 1972 *Flying Scotsman*.
The railway has always been double track, but an unusual feature is that
the two trains each operate on a separate track, with the locomotive running
round the train at each end.
During the mid-1980s the railway was closed for some time to allow for
nearby road improvements, but it was back in operation for the 1987 season.
For the reopening, a new ticket system was introduced. Conventional roll
tickets are issued for single journeys, which are torn in half by the guard
before the train departs. The return tickets are also roll tickets, but printed as
three separate perforated portions. A portion is torn off for each trip made.

A view taken in 1949 of the Cleethorpes Miniat Railway, showing the line's original locomoti a model of the famous *Flying Scotsman*. Notic the vintage style pram.
Courtesy of Humbers Libra

Another view of the *Cleethorpes Flyer* model of Gresley's *Flying Scotsman*, this time seen running tender first alongside the boating lake.
Courtesy A.J. Ludlam

'The train now arriving . . .' One of the three battery-powered diesels hauls its train in Cleethorpes station to pick up its next load of passengers.
Courtesy A.J. Ludl

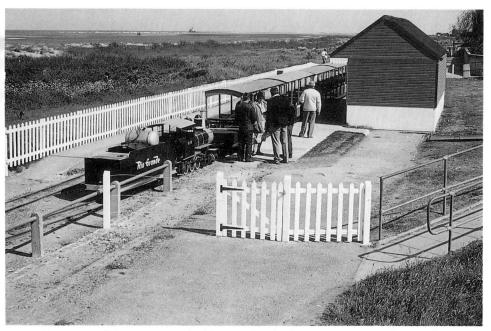

Two views of the new station building on the Cleethorpes Miniature Railway at the town-end of the line on 1st June, 1991 with the 2−8−0 gas hydraulic locomotive built by Severn Lamb in 1972.   *John Edgington*

The Model Railway, Mablethorpe.

A 1930s scene on the Mablethorpe 'Model Railway' with a freelance 4–6–2 locomotive *Lorna Doone*. On this particular trip there seems to be more adults than children! *Courtesy Heyday Publishing*

The 10 in. gauge miniature railway at Mablethorpe featuring the 'Thomas the Tank engine', look-alike guise seen here at Queens Park station in 1988. *Author's Collection*

Towards the end of 1990 it was announced that the Cleethorpes line was to be redeveloped by a new consortium. The unusual 14½ in. gauge would be retained, but the line would be known as 'The Cleethorpes Coast Light Railway', and it was hoped to reintroduce steam locomotives at some future date. A half-mile extension to the line was also planned, along with a new station at the town end of the line.

For some years Cleethorpes had a second miniature railway. This was the 'Wonderland Miniature Railway', situated at the extreme northern end of the promenade. The circular track was situated beneath the Big Dipper at the amusement arcade named 'Wonderland'. The railway was built to a gauge of 7¼ in., and the only reference is in 1971 when a 4−4−4 steam locomotive named *Grimsby Town* was in operation. This had been built in 1955 by a Mr J. Newbutt. An earlier locomotive by the same builder, *Henrietta*, a 4−6−4 of 1947 had been dismantled by 1971.

About 20 miles to the south of Cleethorpes is **Mablethorpe** which has had a miniature railway for well over half a century, though on two different sites.

The first line was built to a gauge of 10¼ in. in the form of a loop around a field in High Street, between George Street and Seacroft Road. Here it was advertised as 'The Model Railway'. It was operated by a freelance 4−6−2 locomotive named *Lorna Doone* which had been built by Lewis Shaw in 1925. It was used at Mablethorpe until the outbreak of war, and was subsequently sold for use on the Hilton Valley Railway, near Bridgnorth, in 1955.

At some time after the war, the line was re-equipped with a pair of Curwen 4−4−2 'Atlantics' which had been built in 1948 for the line at Bognor Regis. They were No. 750 *Blanche of Lancaster*, and No. 751 *John of Gaunt*. Both were sold to inaugurate the Stapleford Miniature Railway near Melton Mowbray in 1958.

It may be that the line closed at this time, as it is understood that a new miniature railway opened in the town in 1962. Meanwhile, the site of the earlier line is now occupied by the Co-op Market Fresh Supermarket.

The present line is believed to have opened in 1962, and is situated in Queens Park, just behind the promenade. The track gauge is said to be 10 in. though one source quotes the railway as being regauged to 7¼ in. in about 1971. The line is in the form of an irregular loop around a putting green, with trains commencing from 'Queens Park Station'. There is a tunnel opposite the station on the opposite side of the loop, and this is used to house rolling stock when the line is not operational. A spur leads into a small shed at the top corner of the circuit, and this houses a spare loco-motive. Sadly, it is said that the line suffers from vandalism each winter.

It is not clear what ran on the railway in the early years. By 1969 a petrol locomotive named *The Dragon*, plus a battery-electric engine were in use. These seem to have been replaced by a petrol locomotive named *Notting-ham Derby* in 1971. The current locomotive is a freelance bogie steam-outline diesel in pale blue livery numbered Ii, and resembles something from 'Thomas the Tank Engine', complete with face! It was said to have been built in 1987 by the operator, but it bears a works plate lettered 'A. Mawby,

The Skegness Miniature Railway operates this freelance diesel named *Ivor*, seen here at the Princes Parade station on a hot Sunday morning in 1988. The author was to be the only passenger on this trip! *Author's Collection*

A 1920s view of the Southend Miniature Railway, note the 3*d.* a ride sign! *Courtesy Heyday Publishing*

Mablethorpe, No. 3 1976'. The tender part of the locomotive is built to resemble an LNER teak coach. All in all, a locomotive well worth seeing!

About 10 miles to the south of Mablethorpe lies the caravan site resort of **Ingoldmells**. Ingoldmells Point was once the location of a short 7¼ in. gauge line which operated only during the height of the holiday season. It was around 100 yards in length, in the form of a continuous loop. Little is known of its history, though the same two locomotives seem to have been in operation for a number of years. *Ingoldmells Flyer* was a 4−6−2 steam replica of the famous LMS 'Princess Royal' class, and was built in 1969, the same year as a Cromar White Bo-Bo petrol locomotive numbered D 7017. Six sit-astride bogie coaches completed the rolling stock of the line.

The exact dates of this line are in doubt. It was certainly in operation between 1960 and 1985, though since that time much redevelopment of the foreshore area has taken place, and today there is no trace of the railway.

The resort of Ingoldmells is also the location of the Skegness Butlins Holiday Camp. This camp was the very first to be opened in the Butlins chain of holiday centres, back in 1936.

Over the years the camp's miniature railway system has been subject to several changes of gauge, and consequently a variety of locomotives has been operated. First on the scene came *Princess Elizabeth*, a Hudswell Clarke 4−6−2, built in 1938. This was a 21 in. gauge locomotive, and had initially been used at the Empire Exhibition in Glasgow before reaching Skegness. It later moved on to Minehead camp, and still later to Pwllheli Holiday Centre.

At some time after the war, the railway was regauged to 15 in., and by the early 1970s a 4−6−2 steam-outline diesel electric locomotive named *Princess Anne* was in use. This had been built by H.N. Barlow in 1953; she was sold in 1976.

By 1980 the line had been replaced by a 2 ft 0 in. narrow gauge line using one of the American-built steam-outline mock Western locomotives which were commonly found at Butlins camps, and the centre is now known as 'Funcoast World'. Under this new identity, even the narrow gauge railway seems to have gone, and in its place appears to be that most diabolical contraption, the 'road train'.

The bracing resort of **Skegness** is our next port of call, and is by far the largest resort on the Lincolnshire coast. The town has a long history of miniature railways, the earliest line dating from the 1920s.

The first line was of 15 in. gauge and was in operation by 1922. The line ran along the seaward side of North Parade from the pier to Pleasureland. The latter end of the line consisted of a balloon loop, and it was here that the stock was housed also. Motive power consisted of a Bassett-Lowke 'Little Giant' class 4−4−2 locomotive *George the Fifth* which had previously worked at Southport and Rhyl. In 1928 the lease on the line was terminated due to redevelopment of the site, and the railway closed. *George the Fifth* moved on to Southend.

On 10th August, 1946, the second miniature railway opened in the resort. This was a 10¼ in. line running along the foreshore from Tower Esplanade. Initially the line used a model of an LMS streamlined 'Coronation' class

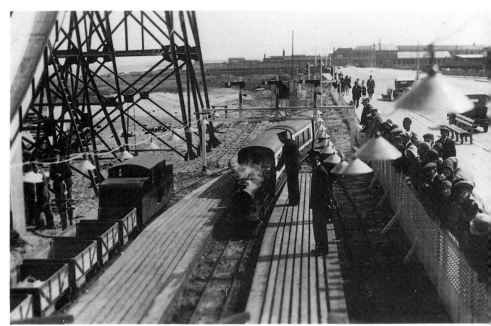

A view of the Great
Yarmouth Miniature
Railway c.1930, taken
from the overbridge at
South Denes station. The
purpose of the pylon to
the left of the railway is
unknown. Note the goods
maintenance train on the
left platform.
*Courtesy Heyday
Publishing*

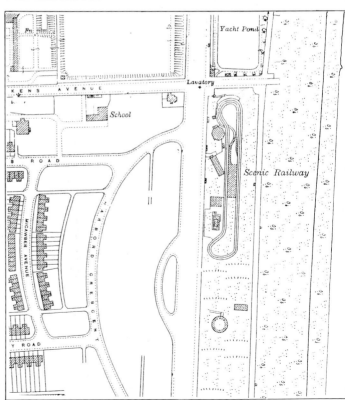

The site of the Great
Yarmouth Miniature
railway under the Scenic
Railway, as shown.
*Reproduced from the
1927, 25" Ordnance
Survey map.*

A quiet day at Hunstanton – even the train driver seems to be looking, perhaps wondering where all his passengers are! The 4–4–0 locomotive is thought to have originated on the Jhansi Railway in India. *Courtesy Wisbech and Fenland Museum*

A commercial postcard view of the 15 in. gauge seaside miniature railway which operated at Great Yarmouth from 1929 to 1937. This view of South Denes station is dominated by the signal gantry. The steam locomotive was a Bassett-Lowke 4–4–2, whilst on the left a petrol locomotive is coupled to a solitary coach.

Oakwood Collection

locomotive which was new the same year, but which had spent the early part of the summer season working at Ayr until the Skegness line was ready for opening. In 1948 a Curwen-built 4−4−2 was working on the line, though whether this was a replacement for the 'Coronation' is not clear. The 'Coronation' moved south to Christchurch in 1952, and was replaced by *Commodore Vanderbilt*, an American-outline 4−6−4 built by Dove of Nottingham. The latter had previously worked on the short line at the summit of the Great Orme in Llandudno. It is not known what became of this second line at Skegness, nor how long it operated.

On 31st March, 1951, the next line opened. This was a 10¼ in. gauge line, the same as the line which operates today, though the present line opened in April 1971. This present line is approximately ¼ mile in length, and runs from Tower Esplanade station parallel to the sea to Princes Parade station. Track is single throughout with a passing loop close to the paddling pool and boating lake. The loop is unusual in that the two tracks are separated by trees, and thus resembles a dual carriageway. Both stations have run-round loops, and these are used on all trips. The joint locomotive and carriage shed is situated at the Princess Parade end of the line.

Details of the line's early motive power are not known, but since the 1970s the line has been diesel operated. A Bo-Bo-Bo locomotive built by Dove of Nottingham was operated in 1971, this being named *The Green Bee*. Other diesels have included *Duplex 2*, a Bo-Bo battery-electric, and 'E 7052', a Cromar White four-wheeled battery locomotive.

Today there are three locomotives. A pair of freelance Bo-Bo diesels in blue livery are named *Fisherman* and *Sea Breeze*. The other locomotive is a narrow gauge style freelance four-wheeled diesel in white livery named *Ivor*. The normal pattern of operation seems to be to use *Ivor* in the mornings, and have two trains in operation in the afternoon using the other two engines.

Carriage stock consists of two sets of four articulated bogie coaches in red livery. Numbers 1 and 4 are covered vehicles, whilst 2 and 3 are open. The second set, numbered 5−8 are all open. The fleet numbers can be found in small figures inside the ends of the coaches.

Around the estuary of The Wash we cross into East Anglia, and the County of Norfolk. For some years a 10¼ in. gauge miniature railway ran on the pier at **Hunstanton**, though its full history is not known due in part to changes of ownership. A photograph exists depicting 'The Pier Miniature Railway, Hunstanton, *c*.1933'. This photograph clearly shows the seaward end of the pier without the pavilion which was destroyed by fire in June 1939, so we must therefore assume that the photograph is post-war rather than pre-war. If this is the case, then the locomotive is probably the Bassett-Lowke 4−4−0 Midland Compound which is thought to have been built in 1928 for the Jhansi Railway in India. After use at Hunstanton it disappeared for some years, before turning up on the Towans Railway at Hayle, in Cornwall.

By 1954 the Hunstanton line was using a Great Western style 4−6−0, believed to be a 'Saint' class locomotive named *Hampton Court*. This had been built by Trevor Guest, and after leaving the resort, eventually turned up at Hastings following a major rebuild. It is subsequently thought to have moved to Melton Mowbray. Rolling stock at Hunstanton at this time consisted of three 12-seater open bogie coaches, and the line was operated by Botterills Amusements.

By 1960 the railway was in the hands of John W. Harris Amusements Ltd, and internal combustion was the order of the day. The locomotive was a rather crude-looking replica of an LNER 'A4' class streamlined Pacific named *Speed Ace*. It is understood that the railway closed down in the early 1960s, and the pier itself was washed away by storms in January 1978.

About 15 miles eastwards along the coast is the small resort of **Wells-Next-The-Sea**. In view of the size of this seaside village, it is surprising to discover that there are two miniature railways. The first of these, the Wells Harbour Railway is unusual in that it replaced a local bus service, which is the opposite of what normally happens.

The 10¼ in. gauge line was opened on 1st July, 1976 and runs for a little under a mile from Wells to a terminus at Pinewood Central which is adjacent to a caravan site near to the beach. The track is single throughout with a passing loop and turntable at each end. During the holiday season, trains run every 40 minutes.

Initially the railway was steam operated using an 0–4–2WT built by D.H. King in 1972, and named *Edmund Hannay*. This was of freelance narrow gauge style, with an open cab. By the summer of 1988, a green diesel locomotive of unknown origin was in use. Carriage stock appears to consist of two open and two covered coaches of the same type, all in maroon livery. All stock is housed at Pinewood Central.

The line was extensively damaged by storms in January 1978, and about ½ mile of track was washed away. Fortunately, the locomotive and rolling stock were away for winter storage, and so escaped damage, but the line was not insured as it is laid on land too prone to flooding for insurance to be guaranteed.

Luckily, the line was rebuilt, and no doubt performs a useful transport function for visitors to the caravan site who might otherwise face a long walk to the shops.

It is believed that the operation of the line has in recent times passed from Commander Francis to another member of his family.

About ¾ mile inland from the quay at Wells is the second of the resorts two miniature railways, the Wells & Walsingham Light Railway. This 10¼ in. line is built on the trackbed of the former Wells–Fakenham standard gauge line which closed in 1964. Fifteen years after the closure, plans were prepared for the building of a new railway, and the line at present runs from a terminus alongside the A 149 Wells to Cromer road for a distance of four miles to the village of Little Walsingham, world-famous for centuries as a centre of pilgrimage to the Shrine of Our Lady at Walsingham.

The railway is believed to be the longest miniature railway of its gauge in the world, and the only 10¼ in. line operating under a Light Railway Order.

Services began in March 1982, and the line became an immediate success, not only with tourists, but with local people too. The line is single track throughout, with sidings and turntables at the two termini. There are two halts *en route* at Warham St Mary and Wighton, and the line passes through pleasant rural country. Close to Little Walsingham is a stretch of line with a gradient of 1 in 29 which has dictated the locomotive requirements of the line. Journey time is 25 minutes each way, and the railway is open daily from Easter to the end of September.

The locomotive stock of the railway consists of three engines, one petrol and two steam. No. 1 *Pilgrim* is an 0−6−0 tank locomotive of freelance narrow gauge style, and was built by David King in 1981. No. 2 *Weasel* is the petrol locomotive which was built by Alan Keef in 1985, and is of 0−6−0 type. Locomotive No. 3 *Norfolk Hero* is by far the most interesting. This is a Garratt 2−6−0+0−6−2 locomotive, probably the only one of 10¼ in. gauge in existence, and was built by Neil Simkins in 1986 with a grant from the English Tourist Board.

Carriage stock originally consisted of five bogie coaches, two of which were enclosed. New carriage stock was added in 1987 to cope with the increased traffic.

In a short time, this railway has achieved a great deal, and its ambition is to extend to Fakenham, about four miles beyond Little Walsingham.

Great Yarmouth is the next stop around the Norfolk coast. From 1929 to 1937 the 15 in. gauge 'Yarmouth Miniature Railway' was in operation, but it is surprising that such a popular resort has not had a miniature line since then.

The line was built by Harold and Nigel Parkinson, and was situated at the South Denes end of the seafront. It ran from a station adjacent to the Pleasure Beach along the beach to South Denes Junction, where the line divided to form a balloon loop, enabling trains to return to the Pleasure Beach. The total length of the line was around 600 yards. The highlight of the system was undoubtedly South Denes station which was unusual on miniature railways in having two island platforms connected by an over-bridge which housed the booking office, waiting room and signal box. An engine shed and turntable were situated at the Pleasure Beach end of the line. Yet another unusual feature of the line was a proper tunnel, 33 yards in length which actually ran underground, instead of the corrugated iron 'mock' tunnels found on so many miniature railways.

To inaugurate the line, the much-travelled Bassett-Lowke 'Atlantic' *Mighty Atom* was obtained from Southport, and was known as *Prince of Wales* at Yarmouth. It was also fitted with smoke deflectors.

This was joined the following year by a two-car petrol-electric railcar set which is thought to have been built by the Parkinsons.

A third unusual item of locomotive stock was a petrol-electric model of an LNER centre-cab electric locomotive, also thought to have been built by the Parkinsons.

Rolling stock consisted initially of a number of goods wagons which were used to carry passengers, but in 1930 three enclosed bogie coaches with doors were built. At one time the railway also ran a dining car service, from which biscuits and lemonade were served to the children.

The main train was hauled by *Prince of Wales* and was known as the 'Yarmouth Belle'. In all aspects, the railway was run to main-line standards wherever possible, and staff also wore correct uniforms.

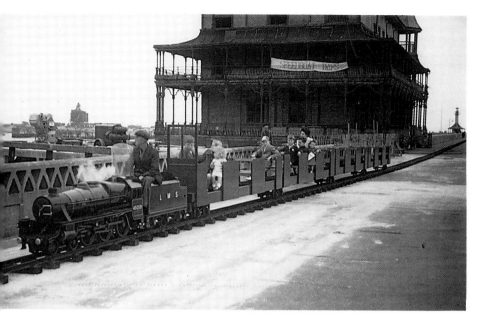

Lowestoft's first miniature railway, seen in June 1953. This line was situated on Claremont Pier, but was moved to the seafront a few years later. Motive power here is a model of a Stanier 'Black Five' 4−6−0 built by Guest.   *H.N. James*

Modern locomotive power in the shape of an Amtrak diesel on the 7¼ in. gauge miniature railway at Pleasurewood Hills American Theme park at Lowestoft.
          Author's Collection

The line closed in 1937, and was sold in its entirety to the Sutton Cold-field Miniature Railway in the Midlands.

A distance of nine miles separates Great Yarmouth from its near neighbour **Lowestoft**, a town which has had several miniature railways.

In the northern outskirts of Lowestoft is Pleasurewood Hills American Theme Park. For an all-in admission charge, one can sample a wide variety of rides and attractions, and make unlimited trips on the two railway systems, one miniature and one narrow gauge, the latter acting as a means of transport around the site.

Construction of the 7¼ in. gauge miniature railway began in October 1981, and the line was formally opened on 22nd May, 1982. At this time, the line was around 1550 yards in length, and in the form of a slightly distorted figure 8. The substantial timber-built station named 'Pleasurewood Hills' also had sidings and a locomotive turntable. The western section of the railway was in woodland, and shortly after the line crossed itself, a short tunnel was situated at the entrance to a long cutting.

By 1985 the miniature railway had been considerably enlarged, and the narrow gauge system added to the much-developed theme park. After leaving the station which is not now named, the train passes a veteran car ride and a satellite weather centre before heading northwards. Before the lake is reached the railway crosses the narrow gauge track, the only place where the two systems make contact. A station was once situated to the north of the lake, though this has now been removed and the site is being re-developed as a haunted magic castle. Just beyond this location is the loco-motive shed, and close by is a two-track tunnel which presumably serves as a stabling point for the carriage stock at night. To the north of the site, the line runs through woodland before turning south again, and on the way back to the station it passes beneath the narrow gauge line.

Initially the track was laid by the owner/operator of the line, but a board near the station states that the trackwork was the work of A.P. Engineering of Great Yarmouth.

The motive power on the miniature railway has changed considerably in the six years since the line opened. Initially the line was worked by two steam and three diesel locomotives. Of the steam engines, *J.M. Cobbold* was the largest. This was a 2−8−4 locomotive, and was a replica of a locomotive built for the Indian State Railway in 1953. Numbered 18282, presumably its date of completion, it was finished in black livery and was named after the owner's bank manager! The other steam locomotive was *Victoria*, a one-third size scale model of a Hunslet Engine Company 0−4−0ST of the type used in the North Wales slate quarries, and was painted in bright blue livery.

The three diesels were *St Paddy*, a replica of the British Rail 'Deltic' locomotive of that name, which was built by the railway, *B.M. Brunning*, a Cromar White model of a BR 'Hymek' locomotive, and *Joy*, a Cromar White battery-electric steeple cab locomotive numbered E7047.

Coaching stock consisted of several rakes of open stock, including a rake of bogie stock complete with windows, and finished in British Rail blue and white livery.

Nowadays, in keeping with the American theme, a pair of Amtrak-liveried diesels provide the motive power. These are numbers 503, *Serendipity*, and

723, B.M. Brunning, neither of which appears to carry a builder's plate. Both are in grey livery with red, white and blue stripes.

Pleasurewood Hills is an enjoyable place to visit complemented by two well-constructed railways.

In Lowestoft itself, the earliest miniature railway is believed to have begun in the early 1950s. This was a 10¼ in. gauge line on Claremont Pier. The locomotive used on this line was a model of a Stanier 'Black Five' class 4–6–0 designed by J.N. Maskelyne and built by Guest of Stourbridge.

In June 1955 a new 10¼ in. line was opened on the seafront, not far from the pier, and the Guest 4–6–0 was transferred from the pier line. This second line was in the form of a circle around a putting green, and was approximately 510 ft in circumference. Two sidings led from the circle, one 110 ft long led to a terminal station, whilst the other, 70 ft in length, led to a turntable and engine shed.

The line was operated by Lowestoft Corporation Publicity & Entertainments Department, and was maintained by the Borough Engineer's Department. Rolling stock consisted of four articulated open bogie carriages, which were rebuilt by the Borough Engineer's Department to give a lower centre of gravity and greater stability on curves.

It is somewhat ironic that the 'Black Five' locomotive, which was numbered 45059 was painted in British Railways green, with the borough coat of arms on the tender.

A change of locomotive took place in 1965, a freelance American 4–4–2 locomotive built by Curwen and numbered 1865 being delivered. The 'Black Five' was sold, and is now at work on a private line in the Midlands. Subsequently, the Curwen locomotive and four articulated open bogie coaches passed into private hands in 1974, though remaining in East Anglia.

The track layout was simplified at an unknown date by the removal of the sidings. The turntable was rescued by the East Suffolk Light Railway at nearby Carlton Colville in 1975 for possible re-use on its narrow gauge line. The Lowestoft line was closed and dismantled by 1980, though the remains of the artificial tunnel can still be seen.

About 4½ miles to the south of Lowestoft is **Kessingland**, a long village stretching almost a mile from the sea inland towards the main A 12 road from Lowestoft to Ipswich. Holiday caravans and camping are a feature of the area. At the main road end of the village is the Suffolk Wildlife & Rare Breeds Park, which was originally opened in 1969. A 10¼ in. miniature railway was added to the park in 1980.

Initially the railway was sited at the north end of the park, and ran for over a mile chiefly in open country, but passing close to woodland on its circuit back to the station. Close to the station are the engine shed and workshops. The railway was extended for the 1987 season, with the trains running south from the original circuit to a new station site close to the shop and cafeteria. This extension has added about ½ mile of track to the circuit.

The initial locomotive stock consisted of a pair of Bo-Bo diesels acquired from the Prestatyn Miniature Railway in North Wales. These had been built around 1972 and were named Conwy Castle and Rhuddlan Castle.

A 2–6–0 tender engine
rounds the neatly tended
lawn on the Felixstowe
Miniature Railway.
Oakwood Collect

The same locomotive with
a fuller load at Felixstowe.
The train is running the
other way round the
circuit this time!
Oakwood Collection

The 0–6–0 *Wendy* on t
spurline at Felixstowe
Miniature Railway.
Oakwood Collect

Since that time, a number of steam locomotives have been introduced. These are E.R. Calthrop, a replica of a Leek & Manifold 2−6−4 built in 1974; Royal Scot, a model of the LMS 4−6−0 of that name, built in 1976; Alice, a 2−6−0 freelance narrow gauge locomotive built in 1984; and Blanche of Lancaster, a Curwen built 4−4−2 of 1948 formerly operated on the Stapleford Miniature Railway. This last locomotive moved in 1988 to the Bickington Steam Railway at Trago Mills, near Newton Abbot in Devon.

The latest acquisition would appear to be Nikki Louise, a freelance 3-axle diesel locomotive in red livery.

Passenger stock originally consisted of two 7-coach sets of articulated bogie coaches from Prestatyn. There are now 16 articulated bogie coaches, made up into four sets, one set of which is enclosed. Non-passenger stock consists of two general purpose goods vehicles.

Travel on the railway is not included in the admission fee to the park. At one time different fare scales were charged, depending on whether steam or diesels were in use; a flat fare is now charged, with no reduced rates for children.

A distance of around 35 miles separates Kessingland from the next miniature railway. The port of **Felixstowe** has in fact two miniature lines close to its seafront. The older of the two, the Felixstowe Miniature Railway has been in operation for a number of years, and is a 7¼ in. gauge line. It is situated on the promenade to the south of the pier, and is in the form of an irregular circle. The railway is well-equipped with a station named 'Felixstowe Lawn Station', and a signal box with semaphore signals. A siding off the main circuit leads to an engine shed complete with turntable. The railway runs round a neatly-cut grass area and attractive flower beds, and is well-maintained.

At one time the line was worked by a pair of steam locomotives, No. 1, Wendy, an 0−6−0T, and No. 2, Rupert, a 2−6−0, both to freelance designs. By 1975, Wendy had been disposed of, and a Cromar White Hymek petrol-driven locomotive had taken its place. A set of articulated bogie coaches make up the passenger stock. In 1986, the locomotive and carriages were repainted in British Rail's Network SouthEast livery to add a modern touch to the line.

At the Peewit Caravan Park in Walton Avenue is a 10¼ in. gauge line which opened in 1974. This line runs along the side of the caravan park, and is 190 yards in length, and includes a 31 ft-long bridge.

The motive power is a steam outline locomotive named Peewit Flyer. This is a petrol locomotive and resembles a Hunslet slate quarry tank locomotive in design.

Clacton-On-Sea is next on our southward journey, where the Butlins Holiday Camp once possessed a 21 in. gauge miniature railway. The motive power was a Hudswell Clarke 'Duchess' class 4−6−2 locomotive built in 1938, and named Princess Margaret Rose. This had originally seen service at the Glasgow Empire Exhibition when new. It was later renamed Queen Elizabeth, and subsequently moved to the camp at Pwllheli. By 1971, the miniature railway had been replaced by a 2 ft narrow gauge line.

Southend Miniature
Railway.
*Reproduced from the
1922, 25" Ordnance
          Survey map.*

A view of the Kursaal
station at Southend
Miniature Railway in
1936, in the background a
Bassett-Lowke class '30'
(formerly *Synolda*)
running on to its train.
          Lens of Sutton

Two views of the Jaywick
Sands Miniature Railway.
The top photograph
shows the train at
Crossways station, whilst
in the bottom view, it will
be noted that the
locomotive is bearing the
name *Century*.
*Courtesy Heyday
Publishing Co.*

The Jaywick Railway's
other locomotive was this
unusual Sentinel oil-fired
locomotive.
Lens of Sutton

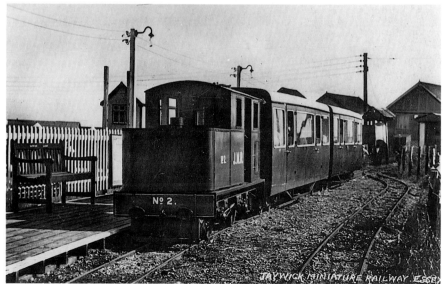

Just to the south of Clacton lies the holiday centre of **Jaywick Sands**, which was once the location of an 18 in. gauge miniature railway. Owned by the Miniature Railway & Specialist Engineering Company, the line was opened on 31st July, 1936 by Mr C.H. Newton, the Divisional General Manager of the Southern Area of the LNER. Flat-bottomed track weighing 12 lb. per yard bolted to steel sleepers was used for the mile-long line, which ran from Jaywick Sands along a dyke to the Tudor Village at Clacton, where the station was known as 'Crossways'. An interesting feature of the line was a 60 ft-long tunnel driven through a prehistoric barrow! One wonders what the Ministry of Public Buildings & Works had to say about this!

To operate the line, there was a model of a Great Northern Railway 'Stirling Single' 4–2–2 locomotive which had been built by Bagnall in 1898, and had operated on the Fairbourne Railway from 1926 to 1936. At one time during its stay at Jaywick it was named *Century*. Problems with the boiler on this locomotive, due to the poor local water, resulted in the engine's replacement by an oil-fired Sentinel locomotive. The subsequent history of the 'Stirling Single' is not known, but it is believed to be intended for use on a new line near Exmouth.

The Jaywick's rolling stock consisted of three luxurious eight-seater bogie coaches complete with electric light. They were painted in an attractive livery of bright green with cream roofs, and had been built especially for the line by Caffyn's of Eastbourne.

The railway closed with the outbreak of World War II, and the Sentinel locomotive and the three carriages were sold to the New Brighton Miniature Railway. The latter then moved in 1965 to the Ravenglass & Eskdale Railway where they were regauged to 15 in. Finally, in 1976, they were resold to the Gloddfa Ganol Narrow Gauge Railway Centre at Blaenau Ffestiniog, where they are preserved.

The small Essex resort of **Maldon** is over ten miles from the open sea, but is situated on the estuary of the River Blackwater. The riverside promenade is the location of a 10¼ in. gauge miniature railway which is approximately 250 yards in length and follows a straight line.

The only locomotive known to have worked on the line is a model of the LMS locomotive *Royal Scot* built by Carland in 1948, and oddly numbered 4716, instead of 6100 or 46100. When the boiler wore out, the locomotive was converted to electric power by means of an electric motor accommodated in the tender. Three bogie coaches made up the passenger rolling stock.

The major holiday resort in Essex is **Southend**, which is famous in railway enthusiast circles for its lengthy pier railway. However, the town also has a place in miniature railway history.

The earliest miniature railway at Southend was at the Kursaal, close to the seafront, and originated around 1920. Of 15 in. gauge, it consisted of 200 yards of straight track, and was operated by a Hershell-Spillman 4–4–0 locomotive with four Bassett-Lowke four-wheeled open coaches.

The line was acquired by Harold and Nigel Parkinson in 1930. They were also operating the line at Great Yarmouth, and, under their management, the Southend line also developed. The line was soon extended to ¼ mile by the addition of a balloon loop, and two new stations were built, 'Lakeside' and 'Central', the latter of which had an overall roof.

The Hershell-Spillman locomotive was retained, and was joined by two further steam locomotives. Bassett-Lowke 'Little Giant' class 4−4−0 George the Fifth (Works No. 18) arrived from Skegness, and a 'mystery' locomotive also from Bassett-Lowke was acquired. This turned out to be class '30' 4−4−2 locomotive Synolda which had been built for the Sand Hutton Light Railway in 1912. It had spent several years in store before coming to Southend. Passenger stock included a five-car enclosed articulated set with vacuum brakes which was designed and built by the Parkinsons.

The line closed in 1938, and the stock was sold to a Mr Dunn of Bishop Auckland.

The Kursaal was again the location of a miniature railway after World War II. This was a 10¼ in. gauge line using a Curwen 4−4−2 steam locomotive of North American appearance, numbered 1149. The railway only ran for a few years, being buried under tons of sand during the 1953 floods which badly affected the east coast.

Away from the Kursaal, two other miniature railways are known to have existed in the resort. The earlier line was of 15 in. gauge, and is thought to have been located somewhere on the seafront, close to the pier. Motive power is believed to have been a Bassett-Lowke 'Little Giant' class 4−4−2 locomotive.

In more recent years, a 10¼ in. gauge line was added to Southend's attractions. This is thought to have opened in June 1977, and was situated close to the boating lake on Marine Parade, not far from the pier, and ran for approximately ¼ mile. The motive power was initially a 2−4−2 steam locomotive built by Viking Locomotives of Sheringham. This was a model of an LNER 'V2' class locomotive, though with a Great Western Railway tender! It was later joined by a petrol-mechanical locomotive with freelance BR diesel locomotive bodywork. Rolling stock consisted of six Cromar White bogie coaches. The line is thought to have closed in 1986.

Our final call in this chapter is at **East Tilbury**, on the northern side of the Thames estuary. A 7¼ in. gauge miniature railway once existed at the Coalhouse Fort in East Tilbury. The line is thought to have been around a mile in length. The rolling stock of this line was of interest as it consisted of a model of a British Rail HST set with 6 coaches, plus a 7-car replica of the ill-fated Advanced Passenger Train, both of which are believed to have been built by Mardyke. Steam locomotives are known to have been used on occasions, and the line closed in 1984 and was dismantled.

Chapter Three
Miniature Railways of South-East England

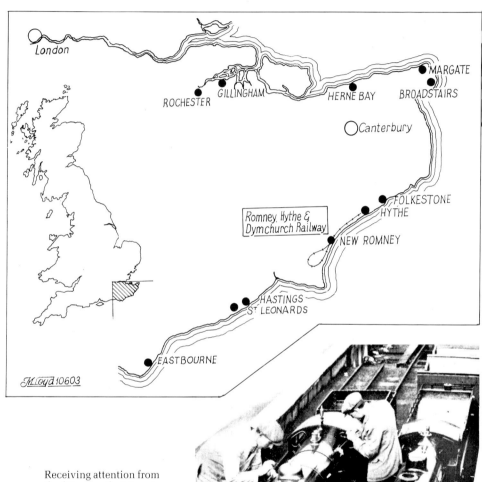

Receiving attention from the fitters on the Margate Dreamland Miniature Railway at Margate is locomotive *Billie*. This was built by Albert Barnes of Rhyl in 1928. On the right is Bassett-Lowke 4–4–2 *Prince of Wales* built in 1909 for the Franco-British Exhibition at White City. The difference in scales is interesting.
Lens of Sutton

Chapter Three
South-East England

ROCHESTER – GILLINGHAM – HERNE BAY – MARGATE –
BROADSTAIRS – RAMSGATE – FOLKESTONE – HYTHE – NEW ROMNEY
– HASTINGS – ST LEONARDS – EASTBOURNE

A little way up the estuary of the River Medway from **Rochester** lies
Upnor Reach. For some years, a 15 in. gauge line known as the Woodland
Park Miniature Railway ran here. One item of motive power which is known
to have worked here is *Michael*, one of the Albert Barnes 4−4−2 locomotives, which was delivered new to this location around 1921.

The neighbouring town of **Gillingham** is situated close to the River
Medway, and at the Strand Lido on the riverbank there exists a 7¼ in. gauge
line. In the mid-1970s the railway comprised an L-shaped track approximately 230 yards in length, running from the Green alongside tennis courts
and a putting green to the Promenade. Rolling stock at this time consisted of
a Bo-Bo petrol-driven locomotive built by Curwen, and four 8-wheeled bogie
coaches. By the mid-1980s, the motive power had changed, and a Mardyke-
built model of a British Rail InterCity 125 was believed to be in operation.
Since that time, the line appears to have been rebuilt or relocated, for it is
now thought to consist of a circular track approximately ¼ mile in length.

The Gillingham area is also thought to have had a second 7¼ in. gauge
line, the Elm Court Miniature Railway, though nothing is known of this line.

The pier at **Herne Bay** is one of the longest in the country, and therefore
needed some form of public transport. A battery-operated tramway was in
use from 1899 until World War II, when it was put out of action, and was not
restored. At a later date, a 7¼ in. gauge miniature railway was established.
One locomotive *Teddy*, a 2−6−0 narrow gauge style model built by Mr J.N.
Liversage of Herne Bay in 1950, was the motive power. This locomotive
subsequently passed to the Hilton Valley Railway, near Bridgnorth, where it
ran as *Hilton Queen*.

The popular resort of **Margate** has had several miniature railways over the
years, though none exists in the town at the present time.

The Dreamland Miniature Railway at Margate was one of the earliest
miniature railways to be established in this country, originating in 1919/
1920. It was designed entirely by Henry Greenly who was becoming famous
in the miniature railway world, and it is believed that he personally super-
vised the work of constructing the 15 in. gauge line.

The original line was in the form of a 600 yds-long loop, and incorporated
four bridges, with a single station named 'Park Station' situated close to
Belgrave Road. Around 1924, the Dreamland site was redeveloped into a fun
fair, and the railway was relaid as a single end-to-end line, Park Station then
being a two platform terminal.

Two steam locomotives are known to have operated at Dreamland, both of
which had interesting histories. The first to arrive was *Prince of Wales*, a
Bassett-Lowke 4−4−2 (Works No. 15 of 1909). This had started life at the
Franco-British Exhibition at London's White City where it was named *Red
Dragon*. It moved to the Rhyl Miniature Railway in 1911, being renamed

The Dreamland Miniature Railway, Margate with two locomotives in the station. Prominent is *Billie*, a 4–4–2 built by Barnes of Rhyl. To the left is the later petrol locomotive.

Courtesy I. Gotheridge

Two views of locomotives used on the Payton Heights Railway, near Margate. *Right* is the 'Western' class locomotive *Lady Sonia*, and *Marie*, an 0–6–0 narrow gauge style locomotive. *Below* is *General Shirley*, an American 'Wild West' style 4–4–0 steam outline diesel locomotive.

Courtesy of A. Pay

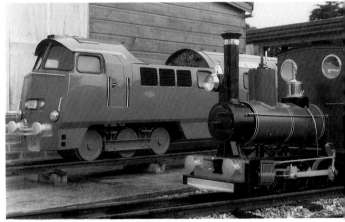

Prince Edward of Wales, and running here until 1920 when it travelled south to Margate. Its career at Dreamland was long-lived, being withdrawn in 1968. Fortunately this interesting locomotive was rescued for preservation.

The second steam locomotive to arrive at Margate was *Billie*, one of the famous Atlantics built by Albert Barnes of Rhyl (Works No. 104 of 1928). This was delivered new to Dreamland, and also had a long career there, being finally withdrawn in 1979. It too has survived, and was brought home to its birthplace by the two men who were striving to save the Rhyl Miniature Railway from extinction. During its retirement, it is known to have worked on the Dudley Zoo Railway around 1982/1983.

Strangely, the two steam locomotives appear to have been numbered in reverse order of acquisition, for *Billie* was numbered 1, and *Prince Edward of Wales* was numbered 2.

In later years, diesel locomotives were added to stock. The first such locomotive was a freelance petrol-driven machine numbered DMR 359. This is understood to have had a Ford car engine, and was new in 1959. A petrol-mechanical locomotive was added in 1975. The rolling stock appears to have consisted of six Bassett-Lowke open bogie coaches which originated at Rhyl.

The Dreamland Miniature Railway closed in 1980.

Proceeding westwards along Margate sea-front, we come to the Old Stone Pier, though it is in fact a stone jetty. A 10¼ in. gauge railway was opened here by the Margate Pier & Harbour Company in 1947, and this ran for about 300 yards along the upper level of the pier between the Droit Office and the Lighthouse. For the first few years the motive power was a model of an LMS Rebuilt 'Royal Scot' class locomotive, probably built by Carland, numbered 1947 and named *Queen of Scots*. By 1952 this had been replaced by a model of a Gresley Pacific named *Flying Scotsman*, and painted in blue livery. Passenger rolling stock consisted of six 20-seater open coaches. It is believed that during the winter seasons, the locomotive was stored in the tunnel at Ramsgate Harbour.

Around 1964 the railway closed, and was re-located on the true Margate Pier, which is known locally as 'The Jetty'. The coaching stock was moved to the new site, but the steam locomotives were replaced by a brand new Curwen-built Bo-Bo 'Western' class diesel locomotive. A fire on the pier in November 1964 is understood to have resulted in the carriage stock falling into the sea – luckily the locomotive was away in winter storage at the time. New bodies were built for the carriages by Curwen & Newbery Ltd of Devizes, and they returned to service.

During 1975 the pier was closed for repairs to be carried out, and the line was dismantled. The track, diesel locomotive and carriages were acquired for use on the Payton Heights Railway, a private line at East Northdown, about 2 miles south-east of Margate. This railway, situated on the property of Mr A. Pay in Green Lane, was technically a private line, but was open to the public on one day each month, and thus deserves mention in this volume.

The 10¼ in. gauge Payton Heights Railway opened in 1976, and consisted of about 900 feet of track, and included a tunnel, a level crossing and a three

A scene on the privately-owned Saltwood Miniature Railway, near Hythe in Kent during one of its public open days. Note the bogie goods vehicle behind the driver.

Courtesy I. Gotheridge

The Romney, Hythe & Dymchurch Railway promoted itself as the 'smallest public railway in the world' for many years. However, it has two larger than average locomotives in the shape of Canadian replicas built by the Yorkshire Engine Company in 1931. One is seen here leaving Hythe at the head of a mixed train.

Oakwood Collection

THE SMALLEST PUBLIC RAILWAY IN THE WORLD, HYTHE.

road engine shed. Rolling stock from the Margate Pier line was joined by a Minimum Gauge Railways 0–6–0 named *Marie*, new in 1975, and a free-lance American style 4–4–0 steam outline diesel locomotive named *General Shirley*. The Margate Curwen Bo-Bo was named *Lady Sonia* whilst at Payton Heights.

Broadstairs is believed to have once had a miniature railway, though no details are known.

Neighbouring **Ramsgate** is also thought to have had a 10¼ in. gauge line on the East Pier at some time in the 1960s, upon which a model of a Western Region diesel locomotive was used.

Between 1950 and 1955, **Folkestone** had a 7½ in. gauge miniature railway on Marine Crescent, at the foot of the cliff lift. This was run by Colonel R.B. Tyrrell who had connections with the Romney, Hythe & Dymchurch Railway. The line was approximately 300 yards in length and ran on land owned by the Folkestone Estates Ltd,

Two locomotives are known to have worked on the line. The regular performer was *Atalanta*, a 0–4–4 tank locomotive built by Tyrrell at New Romney, whilst the other was a Curwen-built model of a Southern Railway 'S15' class locomotive.

About 1970 a short 7¼ in. gauge line was laid on the same site, but did not survive for long. No details of rolling stock are known.

The town of **Hythe** is justly proud of its associations with the Romney, Hythe & Dymchurch Railway, but there was once another miniature railway in the district, though one that is little known. This was the Saltwood Miniature Railway which was a private line situated in the garden of Mr Alexander Schwab's home at Saltwood. Having described it as a private line it should be pointed out that the railway was open to the general public on a number of days each year, and thus it is included in this volume.

The 7¼ in. gauge line originated at Sheffield in 1922, but was moved to Saltwood in 1924. It was first opened to the public in 1931. The track was in the form of a loop, 610 feet in length, and included a tunnel. Passengers were treated to three circuits of the track for their fares which were donated to various charities.

The initial motive power consisted of a 4–4–2 steam locomotive named *Trojan* after a popular make of motor car. This had begun life on the Sheffield line as an 0–4–2T, and was rebuilt in 1928. The second steam locomotive was a 2–6–0 designed by Henry Greenly, but built by Mr Schwab himself in 1938. It was named *Maid of Kent*.

Steam locomotives were displaced in 1970, and *Maid of Kent* was subsequently rebuilt from a Great Western locomotive to a Southern Railway 2–6–0 , and now operates on the Great Cockcrow Railway at Chertsey, in Surrey, bearing the name *River Itchen*.

The line was completely rebuilt in 1975, after which time the line was operated by a pair of Bo-Bo battery-electric locomotives built by T.J. Smith of Lechlade. They were No. 5060 *Earl of Berkeley*, built in 1974, and No. 7007 *Great Western*, new in 1976.

Rolling stock consisted of a four-car articulated open bogie set, two sit-astride coaches, plus two enclosed coaches, one of which was formerly a

A good general view of Hythe station on the Romney, Hythe & Dymchurch Railway.
Lens of Sutton

A view looking into the station buildings at Hythe with the stock being moved into the
covered station ready for service. *Lens of Sutton*

diesel locomotive on a garden railway at Lechlade.

Because the Saltwood Miniature Railway pre-dated the Romney, Hythe & Dymchurch Railway, it once laid claim to being the world's oldest purpose-built miniature railway. It seems to have closed in recent years.

Although the **Romney, Hythe & Dymchurch Railway**'s history has been widely told, no survey of seaside miniature railways can ignore a system of this size, being one of the few miniature railways in this country to be authorised by a Light Railway Order. The Romney, Hythe & Dymchurch is also the longest miniature railway in Britain, at 13⅞ miles.

The line originated out of the friendship between J.E.P. Howey, and Count Louis Zborowski who were both interested in motor racing as well as miniature railways. It was their ambition to build and operate a miniature railway to main line standards. An attempt to buy and develop the Ravenglass & Eskdale Railway failed, and so they were forced to look elsewhere for land upon which to build their dream railway. The partnership came to an abrupt end when Zborowski was killed in October 1924 whilst driving in the Monaco Grand Prix. Howey eventually decided to proceed with his ideas for a miniature railway which would act as a memorial to Zborowski.

Henry Greenly was set to work in 1925 to locate a suitable site for the line. Two possibilities presented themselves. One at Brean Sands in Somerset was considered, but eventually ruled out because it was felt that there would be insufficient trade for the line. The second alternative was suggested by the Southern Railway. Powers had been obtained to build a standard gauge line between New Romney and Hythe, but had not been proceeded with. At a meeting in September 1925, Howey decided that this was the location he wanted, and so plans were drawn up by Greenly, and a Light Railway Order was sought. There then followed several months of negotiations and inquiries before the Order was finally confirmed on 26th May, 1926.

Once permission for the line was granted, Howey turned his attention to locomotives. He already had two Pacifics which had been ordered by his late colleague, Zborowski, and these were named *Green Goddess* and *Northern Chief*. Within a short space of time, he ordered a further five identical locomotives, though not all materialised as Pacifics, these being named *Southern Maid, Hercules, Samson, Typhoon,* and *Hurricane.* Also acquired was an unusual German-built Krauss 0–4–0T with tender, which Howey named *The Bug.*

The line was formally opened on Saturday 16th July, 1927 by the Lord Warden of the Cinque Ports. At this time, the line ran from Hythe to New Romney, a distance of around 8 miles. The railway was an immediate success, and Howey lost no time in planning an extension of the tracks a further 5 miles to Dungeness. The Board of Trade approved this extension on 12th July, 1928 though the line had already been built and had been in use as far as The Pilot since May! The final stretch of track from The Pilot to Dungeness opened in August 1928.

With the railway now open to its full extent, it was decided that two more locomotives were needed. Two were ordered from Davey Paxman, the supplier of the earlier ones, but these were soon cancelled. Instead, Howey decided that these should be built by the railway at New Romney. In order to

Burmarsh Road on the Romney, Hythe & Dymchurch Miniature Railway, with two trains passing in 1934.

R.W. Kidner

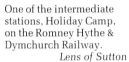

One of the intermediate stations, Holiday Camp, on the Romney Hythe & Dymchurch Railway.

Lens of Sutton

Another good general view of the busy terminus at Hythe station on the Romney, Hythe & Dymchurch Miniature Railway.

R.W. Kidner Collection

overcome the problem of insufficient winter protection for the driver, it was decided to construct replicas of Canadian locomotives which had more enclosed cabs. These were finally completed by the Yorkshire Engine Company in 1931, and were named *Doctor Syn* and *Black Prince*. Strangely enough, the two new locomotives saw little use on winter trains, as an ugly internal combustion locomotive was constructed, and this propelled winter trains on the line until the start of World War II. The only other locomotive development in the pre-war period was the sale of *The Bug* in November 1933.

When war broke out in September 1939, the railway immediately went over to a winter service, and before long, troop trains were running on the railway to premises acquired by the armed forces. As the possibility of invasion grew closer, the beaches were barricaded and placed out-of-bounds, and service on the railway ceased by April 1940. The Somerset Light Infantry took over control of the line in June 1940, and based at Dymchurch, began preparations for operating an armoured train. This was subsequently hauled by *Hercules* which was kept in steam at all times. As the war progressed, the Royal Engineers took over the line, but ceased to have any use for it by the spring of 1944.

In July 1945 Howey gained control of the line once more, and it was immediately clear that it would take a good deal of time to restore the line to anything like its pre-war standard. Not to be outdone, he regauged about a mile of track around New Romney to 10¼ in. upon which he ran an 0–6–0T locomotive which he had acquired back in 1938.

The first section of the railway to be reopened was between Hythe and New Romney which took place on 1st March, 1946. Much of the reconstruction work had been done by German prisoners-of-war. The result of the reopening was a vast influx of visitors, and this brought about a desperate need for new rolling stock. By mid-summer 1946 the line was open to Maddiesons Camp, and by early the following year the full line to Dungeness was once again in use. In order to expedite the overhauling of the locomotive fleet, three engines were dealt with by the Southern Railway at Ashford Works.

The 1950s and early 1960s saw few developments on the railway as a decline set in, and Captain Howey, the line's owner, died in September 1963. Following his death, the line was sold to two retired bankers who ran the railway for four years. During their period of management, a new refreshment room was built at New Romney, and the track layout at the station was also improved.

The next owners inherited major problems when they took over in 1968. A report showed that major reconstruction of several bridges on the line was needed, and this was carried out between 1968 and 1971. There was also a major reorganisation of the workshops at New Romney. 1969 saw an abortive plan to move the railway to Devon, to be rebuilt on the track-bed of the Goodrington to Kingswear line, but the present Dart Valley Railway laid prior claim to the site.

An accident at a level crossing in 1973 resulted in the death of an engine driver. This renewed the question of safety on the line, and in consequence, five level crossings were equipped with automatic flashing warning lights.

In 1976 an additional locomotive was acquired. This was one of a trio built by Krupp in 1937 for an exhibition railway at Dusseldorf, though they were later used on a line at Cologne. This line closed in the 1960s, and two locomotives were obtained for use at Bressingham Gardens in Norfolk. The third locomotive, which had disappeared for some years was brought to New Romney where it was overhauled and named *Black Prince*.

At about the same time, major reconstruction of New Romney station took place, and these alterations included an overall roof which provided shelter not only for passengers, but also provided useful under-cover storage for spare carriage stock.

In 1977 a daily school train was introduced. This ran from Burmarsh Road station, which was specially reopened, to New Romney and conveyed around 200 children attending Southlands Comprehensive School; the train was appropriately named *The Southlandian*.

As the years progressed, there was growing concern at the decline in passenger traffic on the line, a decline which was reflected in the gradual reduction in visitors generally throughout the south-east. At that time, no financial assistance was available from local or central government. Later, the local authority agreed to assist the railway by funding a new diesel locomotive. Design work commenced in late 1977, but construction was not proceeded with, as the railway felt that a diesel locomotive would not be in keeping with the railway's image.

Compared with the historical and engineering importance of the railway, the scenic attractions are less favourable. In general, the route is flat and largely uninteresting in contrast to the Ravenglass & Eskdale Railway. Travelling southwards from the terminus at Hythe, there are stations at Burmarsh Road, Dymchurch, Jefferstone Lane, New Romney, Romney Sands and Dungeness, plus several intermediate halts which are not observed by most trains. Beyond New Romney, the line runs close to the sea, and the terminus at Dungeness has the added attraction of a lighthouse close by. Unfortunately, a large nuclear power station is also in the vicinity which detracts from the appeal of the area.

The main attraction on the line is undoubtedly New Romney, where the locomotive and carriage sheds are situated. There is also an excellent souvenir and book shop, and an impressive model railway exhibition.

The future of the line is very much in question at the present time. Proposed road developments in the area could spoil the appeal of the line, and consideration is being given to extending the railway by four miles to reach the British Rail main line at Sandling. This would add a section of pleasant scenery and perhaps enable the line to continue being a popular local attraction.

The steam locomotives used on the line are as follows:

No. 1   *Green Goddess* 4−6−2 Davey Paxman (Works No. 15469).
No. 2   *Northern Chief* 4−6−2 Davey Paxman (Works No. 15470).
No. 3   *Southern Maid* 4−6−2 Davey Paxman (Works No. 16040).
       Dates Built: Nos. 1 & 2 (1925), No. 3 (1926). Driving wheels: $25\frac{1}{2}$ in. diameter. Boiler pressure: 180 lb per sq.inch. Cylinders: $5\frac{1}{4}$ in. × $8\frac{1}{2}$ in. Overall length: 22 ft $10\frac{1}{2}$ in. Weight: 7.85 tons. Current liveries: Nos. 1 & 3 (Great Northern green), No. 2 (Napier green).

No. 4   *The Bug* 0–4–0 tank locomotive with tender. Krauss (Works No. 6378).
Date built: 1926. Driving wheels: 15¾ in. diameter. Boiler pressure: 180 lb
per sq.inch. Cylinders: 4 and nine-sixteenths inches × 6 and five-sixteenths
inches. Weight: 5.1 tons.

No. 5   *Hercules* 4–8–2 Davey Paxman (Works No. 16041).

No. 6   *Samson* 4–8–2 Davey Paxman (Works No. 16042).
Date built: 1927. Driving wheels: 19½ in. diameter. Boiler pressure: 180 lb
per sq.inch. Cylinders: 5¼ in. × 8½ in. Overall length: 23 ft 7¾ in. Weight:
8.25 tons. Current liveries: No. 5 (bright red), No. 6 (black).

No. 7   *Typhoon* 4–6–2 Davey Paxman (Works No. 16043).

No. 8   *Hurricane* 4–6–2 Davey Paxman (Works No. 16044).
Date Built: 1927. Driving wheels: 25½ in. diameter. Boiler Pressure: 180 lb
per sq.inch. Cylinders: 5¼ in. × 8½ in. Overall length: 22 ft 10½ in.
Weight: 8.1 tons. Current liveries: No. 7 (Malachite green), No. 8 (Cale-
donian blue).

No. 9   *Winston Churchill* 4–6–2 Yorkshire Engine Co. (Works No. 2294).

No. 10 *Dr. Syn* 4–6–2 Yorkshire Engine Co. (Works No. 2295).
Date built: 1931. Driving wheels: 25½ in. diameter. Boiler pressure: 180 lb
per sq. inch. Cylinders: 5¼ in. × 8½ in. Weight: 8.75 tons. Current liveries:
No. 9 (red), No. 10 (black).

No. 11 *Black Prince* 4–6–2 Krupp (Works No. 1664).
Date built: 1937. Cylinders: 5⅞ in. × 9¾ in. Overall length: approx. 26 ft.
Weight: 7.2 tons. Current livery: black.

The railways first diesel locomotive entered service in 1984. This is No. 12 *John Southland*, a Bo-Bo machine built by TMA Engineering, and powered by a Perkins 6 cylinder 112 hp engine. Overall length: 21 ft 0 in. Weight: 5.9 tons. Current livery: dark red.

No. 14 a similar locomotive to No. 12, built 1989. In Canadian Pacific livery of yellow and grey.

The carriage stock consists of between 60 and 70 vehicles of various types, each individual type being numbered in a separate sequence. There is also a quantity of goods stock.

The territory served by the Romney, Hythe & Dymchurch Railway has also seen five other miniature railways in its midst over the years, though none has been a competitor, for all five have had connections with the RH&DR.

New Romney had a second miniature railway for a number of years. This line resulted from Henry Greenly's departure from New Romney, and the purchase of the latter's bungalow in 1927 by Colonel Tyrrell. The Colonel was granted a piece of land by Captain Howey of the Romney, Hythe & Dymchurch Railway upon which to build a short line. The land was situated about ¼ mile east of New Romney Station, and the new line was built to a 7¼ in. gauge, and was around 600 yards long.

Two locomotives are known to have worked on the line, the first being a freelance 4–4–0 built by the Colonel himself. This proved to be inadequate to haul the six open bogie coaches, and so Tyrrell designed and built an 0–4–4T named *Atalanta* to replace it.

The railway operated for several seasons up to the outbreak of the war, when the two locomotives were put into store.

The Dymchurch area was next to see another miniature railway. In 1938, a short 10¼ in. gauge line was laid at Dymchurch, and this used equipment

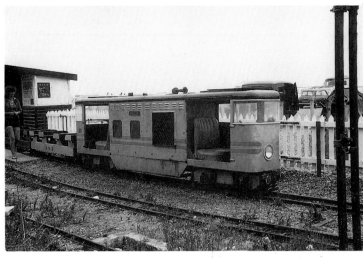

Diesel locomotive *Uncle Jim* seen here at the station (opposite East Cliff) on the Hastings Miniature Railway on 14th July, 1983.

D. Gou

A Great Western locomotive on the Sussex coast! For a time the Hastings Miniature Railway operated this superb model of a 'Saint' class 4−6−0. Here, 2943 *Hampton Court* is seen backing onto its train.

H. James

On the beach at Hastings is *Firefly*, a much-rebuilt locomotive which was originally built in 1934. the cab is Jim Hughes, the line's operator.

Courtesy I. Gotheric

from the late H.C.S. Bullock's line at Farnborough. It is not clear how long it remained in operation, but motive power was in the hands of an 0–6–0 pannier tank which Bullock himself had built.

In 1945, Colonel Tyrrell returned to railway operation and was persuaded by Captain Howey to change to a 10¼ in. gauge; as a result, he laid out a short line alongside Dymchurch Station. On this line he ran a 4–6–0 'Royal Scot' locomotive with six articulated bogie coaches. The line was not a success and only ran for a couple of years.

By the end of the war, the Romney, Hythe & Dymchurch Railway was in no position to operate a service due to years of neglect and wartime damage, and so in order to provide a train ride for the few visitors that season, the down line between the engine sheds at New Romney and the Warren bridge was regauged to 10¼ in. simply by moving one rail inwards. This line only operated in August and September 1945, and the trains were run with the Bullock 0–6–0 pannier tank and stock which had been used at Dymchurch in 1938.

After a brief spell of running a miniature railway at Folkestone, Colonel Tyrrell returned to the Romney area, and built a 10¼ in. gauge line on the shore between Littlestone and Greatstone. The 'Royal Scot' locomotive was brought out of storage and, together with a second-hand 4–4–2, the railway proved a success. Unfortunately, following a minor accident when a boy was injured by the train, the line was ordered to be closed down.

Leaving the Romney Marsh area, and continuing our journey westwards along the coast we come to **Hastings**. The first miniature railway in the district was opened in 1947 at **St Leonards**. This was a 10¼ in. gauge line owned by the Ian Allan Organisation. The line was only short, and operated on the beach. In this location, it ran for only one season, being transferred to neighbouring Hastings in 1948 where it remains to this day.

The Hastings site is at the eastern end of the seafront. Initially the line was 250 yards long, but extensions around 1950, and again in 1959 make the line around ½ mile in length today.

The western end of the line is at Marine Parade Station, close to the children's boating lake. The station has a single platform and run-round loop. Leaving the station, the track passes the Go-Kart circuit before an unnamed station at the Lifeboat House is reached. A passing loop is situated here. Beyond this intermediate halt, the track singles once more, passing alongside the coach park and then beside the famous wooden net huts. Shortly before the eastern terminus at Rock-a-Nore is reached, the line passes through an artificial tunnel which also acts as the engine shed. The eastern station is a two-track terminus.

The rolling stock for both the St Leonards and Hastings lines had been purchased from Lord Downshire's private line at Easthampstead Park, and included a fine-scale model of the original LMS 'Royal Scot' class locomotive No. 46100 which had been built by Bassett-Lowke in 1938. Also used at Hastings for a time was a model of a Great Western 'Saint' class 4–6–0 locomotive. This was No. 2943 *Hampton Court* which is believed to have been originally built by Trevor Guest but had been reconstructed over the years. The third steam locomotive at Hastings was also noteworthy. This was *Firefly* originally built by H.C.S. Bullock in 1934 as an 0−6−0 pannier tank, it had been rebuilt in 1946 as an 0−6−0 tender engine.

Unfortunately, in recent years the steam locomotives have been replaced, and the railway currently operates a green double-ended diesel locomotive, believed to have been built by Shepperton. It is named *Uncle Jim* after the late Jim Hughes who had managed the line for many years.

For some years, Hastings has had a second miniature railway. There was once a 10¼ in. gauge line in Alexandra Park, a long 120 acre park about ¾ mile inland from the pier. The line would seem to have been operated by the Ian Allan Organisation for the line's motive power consisted of *Meteor IV*, a 2−4−2 diesel locomotive built at Shepperton in the 1960s. The line was certainly in operation in 1971 but had gone by 1980.

On 24th April, 1981, the East Sussex Model Engineers opened their miniature railway in Alexandra Park. This is a multiple gauge system with tracks of 3½ in., 5 in. and 7¼ in. gauge. The line is around 400 feet long, and includes a tunnel.

The genteel resort of **Eastbourne** is our last visit in this chapter. The town had a 7¼ in. gauge miniature railway for some years, but this had closed by 1971. The location of the line is not known, but two steam locomotives are believed to have worked there. No. 6309 was a 2−6−0 built by a firm named Wilson, whilst *Gloster* was an 0−4−0T possibly from the same manufacturer.

The 7¼ in. gauge New Romney Miniature Railway ran for some years up to the Second World War. Situated close to the Romney, Hythe & Dymchurch Railway, the line was run by Col. Tyrrell whose 0−4−4 tank locomotive *Atalanta* is seen here with a train of over-dressed passengers.   *Courtesy of the K. Taylorson Collection*

The rural setting of the 10¼ in. gauge line in Hotham Park, Bognor Regis. The line was owned and run for a time by the Ian Allan organisation, and the freelance diesel locomotive was a product of their Shepperton works.　　　　*Courtesy M. Simpson*

We return to Hastings for this photograph of *Royal Scot* built by Bassett-Lowke. It had started life on a private railway at Easthampstead Park. The building behind the locomotive is one of the famous wooden net huts, so much a feature of the Hastings seafront.　　　　*Oakwood Collection*

Miniature Railways of South-Central England

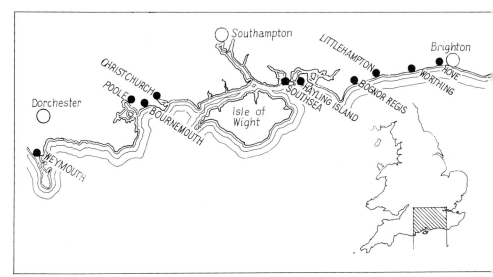

Based on the class '52' Western Diesel-Hydraulic design, *Western Comet* runs round the lake on the Brooklands Miniature Railway at East Worthing. *Author's Collection*

Chapter Four
South-Central England

HOVE – WORTHING – LITTLEHAMPTON – BOGNOR REGIS – HAYLING
ISLAND – SOUTHSEA – STOKES BAY – ISLE OF WIGHT –
CHRISTCHURCH – BOURNEMOUTH – POOLE – WEYMOUTH

Our starting point for this chapter is Brighton which surprisingly does not
seem to have had a miniature railway. Perhaps such a form of transport is
considered too mundane for this grand historic resort which still has the
pioneering Volk's Electric Railway on its seafront, and which once had the
Brighton & Rottingdean Seashore Electric Tramway – an eccentric electric
tramway which ran in the sea.

Neighbouring **Hove** had a 10¼ in. gauge line at the King Alfred Amusement Centre on the seafront during the 1970s. Motive power consisted of a
four-wheeled battery-electric locomotive with steam outline bodywork of
unknown origin.

Next along the coast is **Worthing**, where at the Brooklands Pleasure Park
in East Worthing is the Brooklands Miniature Railway. There have been two
miniature lines here over the years, the first being a 9½ in. gauge line which
is believed to have been steam operated. This was replaced by a new 10¼ in.
gauge line in 1965. This is ¾ mile in length, and runs around the perimeter
of an ornamental lake. The initial motive power on this second line is not
known, but the current locomotive is a Severn Lamb 'Western' class Co-Co
locomotive named *Western Comet* in red livery, which has been in operation
since 1967.

A three-track shed close to the station houses the locomotive and stock
which consists of five 6-seater open bogie coaches numbered 1 to 5. Trains
run every 20 minutes throughout the day during the summer season, and un-
titled roll tickets are issued for all passengers.

A few miles west of Worthing is **Littlehampton**. At the eastern end of the
Common is situated the Littlehampton Miniature Railway which runs for
about half a mile to Mewsbrook Park. The line is unique in Britain in having
a gauge of 12¼ in. The track is single throughout, with a two-track terminus
at each end.

Opened in 1948, the line initially had two 4–6–4 freelance steam locomotives with an interesting history. They were designed by H.C.S. Bullock,
and built around 1933 as 10¼ in. gauge 4–6–4T locomotives for the Surrey
Border & Camberley Railway, and were rebuilt to their present form in 1939.
At Littlehampton, they are numbered 1005 and 2010, and are in green livery,
though unnamed.

By 1975, the locomotive stud had been increased to five. Little is known of
a 4–4–2 Atlantic named *Prince Edward*, but this had gone by 1980. The two
other locomotives were acquired from the Bognor Pier Railway, and were
steam-outline locomotives, one being an 0–4–2 petrol machine, the other a
2–4–2 battery-electric. These were numbered 3015 and 4020 respectively.

Rolling stock consists of ten open bogie coaches. The engine shed and
workshops are situated at the Mewsbrook Park terminus.

Beyond the estuary of the River Arun we come to the West Sussex resort of
Bognor Regis, which has had several miniature railways over the years,
though none has proved a lasting success.

The first line lasted for only one season, 1909. This was a 10¼ in. gauge line owned and constructed by a Mr R.W. Briggs. The location of the line and its length are not recorded. The locomotive used was *Winnie*, a 4−4−0 built by Mr Briggs' father between 1906 and 1908. Three open coaches made up the rolling stock. Mr Briggs (Junior) went on to an apprenticeship at Derby Locomotive Works at the end of the summer season, and so the line was closed and moved back to the family home at Harpenden in Hertfordshire, where it remained until 1913.

The railway returned to the area again in 1913. Mr Briggs (Senior) retired that year and moved to a house at Shripney, about two miles inland from the resort. Here *Winnie* was used on a circuit of track in the family's garden, and was in use each summer until 1956 giving rides to local children and visitors. The entire railway was presented to the Chichester & District Society of Model Engineers in 1963 and was finally reopened at their headquarters in 1978.

Back in Bognor Regis itself, the next line was laid in the 1940s, and was owned by Southern Miniature Railways of Southsea who had moved the line from its original home at Stokes Bay, Gosport. The railway was sold to another operator in 1951 and was dismantled by the late 1950s when the site was acquired for a new Butlin's Holiday Camp.

Two locomotives used in the early period of the railway were a pair of Curwen–built 4−4−2 Atlantics based on Canadian Pacific prototypes. They were No. 5718 *Blanche of Lancaster* and No. 751 *John of Gaunt*. They were later sold for use at Mablethorpe, and are still in existence, though now at Stapleford Park in Leicestershire, where *Blanche of Lancaster* is now numbered 750.

In 1971, the Ian Allan Organisation established a 10¼ in. gauge line in Hotham Park, a few minutes walk inland from the Promenade. Much of the track for this line came from a short-lived railway at Bassett's Manor, Hartfield, Sussex. To operate the Hotham Park line, Shepperton Metal Products delivered a new diesel-mechanical locomotive named *Meteor II*. This was later joined by a similar locomotive named *Meteor III*.

The railway changed hands after the 1974 season, and is currently run by Arun District Council by whom it is marketed as the 'Woodland Miniature Railway'. Operation is understood to be daily between Easter and October, though no details are known of the current rolling stock.

The Ian Allan Organisation also operated a second line in the resort from 1970 to 1975. This was situated at Beaulieu Gardens on the Esplanade. This was a 7¼ in. gauge line, and was operated by a Shepperton Metal Products four-wheeled diesel locomotive named *Thunderbolt*. Redevelopment of the seafront caused the railway to be dismantled in 1976, and stored for future use.

Yet another line in the town existed on the pier. This would seem to have been built in the mid-1960s, and used two locomotives which had moved to the Littlehampton Miniature Railway by 1975. They were both steam-outline, one being an 0−4−2 petrol machine dating from around 1966, whilst the other was a 2−4−2 battery electric dating from 1969.

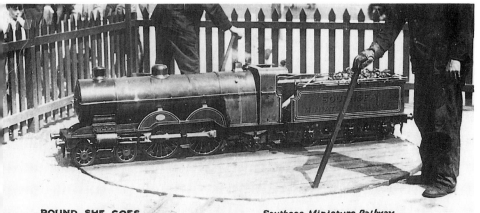

ROUND SHE GOES.   *Southsea Miniature Railway.*

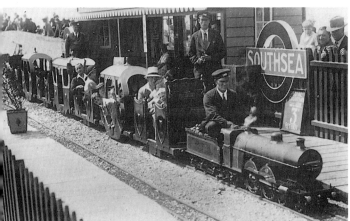

Three illustrations
depicting the Southsea
Miniature Railway in its
early days. The loco-
motive is a Bassett-Lowke
4–4–2. Notice the
unusual covered
carriages. There are plenty
of spectators – were they
all waiting for a ride
perhaps?
Oakwood Collection

HERE WE GO.   *Southsea Miniature Railway*

The most recent miniature railway to open in the Bognor Regis area is at the former Butlin's Holiday Camp, now known as 'South Coast World'. A 12 in. gauge line is thought to have opened here in June 1987, though no further details are known.

On the west side of Chichester Harbour is the large peninsula known as **Hayling Island**. This is a popular holiday centre with many caravans and chalets. The earliest miniature railway to operate here was around 1930, when what is thought to have been a 12 in. gauge line was in operation. Two locomotives are known to have worked here – a model of a Great Northern Railway 4–4–2, and a freelance 4–6–2 which is thought to have moved to Southsea after the Second World War.

During the 1970s, a 10¼ in. gauge line was operating in the district. Two steam locomotives are known to have been used, both having interesting histories. A 4–4–4 locomotive which had originated around 1909 as a 4–4–2 on a private line near Stourbridge where it had been known as *John Terence* was in use along with *Bubbles*, a 4–6–4 built by Bullock in 1936 for a private line. The miniature railway at Hayling Island subsequently closed, and some years later was replaced by a 2 ft 0 in. narrow gauge line known as the East Hayling Light Railway at the Mill Hythe Holiday Village, though this too has since closed.

Across Langstone Harbour to the west of Hayling Island is Portsea Island, which forms the city of Portsmouth, and its seaside resort of **Southsea**. Southsea has a long history of miniature railways dating back to the 1920s, and it is thought to have had no fewer than four lines since then.

The first railway to be opened is said to have begun in 1924. This was a 9¼ in. gauge line situated on Southsea Common, at the western end of the resort. The line was owned by the local authority and consisted of approximately ¾ mile of track in the form of a single line with a balloon loop at one end, and a station with a run-round loop at the other. Mystery surrounds the early locomotive stock, but it may have been a model of a Great Northern Railway Atlantic 4–4–2. By about 1930, the rolling stock of the private railway at Littleton Park, Shepperton had been acquired and was in use. This consisted of a Bassett Lowke 'Great Northern' Atlantic 4–4–2 locomotive built in 1924 and named *Sir Edward Nicholl* after its previous owner, plus a rake of elaborate open and closed carriages. The first Southsea line closed with the outbreak of war in 1939.

After the war, Southsea became the headquarters of Southern Miniature Railways Ltd, and in time they operated a trio of 10¼ in. gauge lines. The first Southsea line was rebuilt and regauged to 10¼ in., and in its new guise included a short tunnel. The railway was run by two 4–4–2 steam locomotives built by the company. These were No. 1002 *Valiant* and No. 1003 *Victory*. By the 1970s, the line had been dieselised with two locomotives also built by the company. These were D108, a Co-Bo diesel locomotive powered by a Ford engine, and *Avenger*, a Bo-Bo locomotive with a Triumph engine.

By 1977, the 10¼ in. gauge line had been dismantled, and in that year, a new line had been built on the site, unique in British miniature railway history in being of 17 in. gauge. The track was single throughout with no sidings or loops. The motive power for the new line was equally unusual, for it was a Belgian-built Bo-Bo battery-electric steam-outline locomotive new in 1976. Its method of operation was different too, for the driver controlled the train from the front seat of the leading coach, which enabled one passenger to sit in the locomotive cab! Three toast-rack open bogie coaches made up the rolling stock of this unusual line which unfortunately only lasted until 1984.

However, this was not the end of the Southsea miniature railway story, for yet another line was laid on the site. This fourth line appeared around 1988, and was once again of 10¼ in. gauge. The main terminus was adjacent to the new Portsmouth Sea Life Centre. Rolling stock consisted of a freelance diesel locomotive in blue and yellow livery, plus an 0–6–0 steam tank locomotive. Carriage stock consisted of a number of red-liveried sit-astride vehicles. This railway too was a short-lived one, and closed in 1989, and was moved in its entirety to the Royal Victoria Country Park at Netley, near Southampton. Two reminders of this last line remain at Southsea however – the booking office complete with name boards, and picture postcards depicting the railway on sale at numerous outlets in the resort.

The beach close to Southsea's Clarence Pier forms a convenient departure point for the hovercraft service to the Isle of Wight, and we will cross the Solent here also to look at the island's sole miniature railway, and at ambitious plans for a line which never materialised.

The Sandham Castle Mini Railway at **Sandown** on the south-east corner of the island is situated in a children's play area on Culver Parade, and the track is laid to a gauge of 10¼ in. It would appear to have originated around 1969, and has operated since then using a Shepperton-built 2–4–2 diesel locomotive appropriately named *Sandham Castle*. In the early years the line was run by the Ian Allan Organisation. In addition, a pair of Co-Bo petrol-mechanical locomotives are in stock, these having been built by Southern Miniature Railways. They are No. D108 *Vanguard*, and No. 608. The track is in the form of a continuous loop, 300 yards in length. Rolling stock consists of six open bogie coaches.

Although this book is primarily concerned with seaside miniature railways which have existed, it does not seem entirely unreasonable to include one which was seven years in the planning stages, and still came to nothing.

The line concerned was the Medina Valley Railway. This was to have been a 15 in. gauge line linking Newport and Cowes along the track-bed of a closed standard gauge branch, and would have been approximately 3 miles long. Planning began in 1975, and it was hoped to operate a half-hourly service using two trains. There was local opposition to the plan on the grounds that the line would cause a nuisance and noise. However, these objections were overcome, and a Light Railway Order allowing the line to be built was granted in November 1980.

During 1981 it was hoped to buy the track and stock of the Fairbourne Railway for use on the Medina Valley Railway, but this fell through. It had been hoped to start work on construction in late 1981 for opening in 1982. The County Council gave the promoters until the end of 1982 to show they

A superb view of the Littlehampton Miniature Railway in 1960. The line had the unusual gauge of 12½ in. Both locomotives were built for the now closed Surrey Border & Camberley Railway. *E. Wilmhurst*

Circling the lake on the 10¼ in. gauge Poole Park Miniature Railway is this freelance 4–4–2 locomotive named *Vanguard* which ran until 1965. *Courtesy I. Gotheridge*

could finance the line, and when that date passed, the County Council began to consider plans for a cycleway along the route instead.

Back over on the mainland, we visit **Stokes Bay**, south of Gosport. This was the location of the first line run by Southern Miniature Railways Ltd, who began the line in 1946. Little else is recorded about this line, except that it is known to have been moved to Bognor Regis after only a short time.

Moving on westwards, our next venue is the town of **Christchurch**, which had a miniature railway for a number of years, though this is no longer in existence.

The 10¼ in. gauge line was situated at the Quay, and consisted of about ½ mile of track in the form of a circle. Leaving the station, trains ran along the edge of a car park, down the side of Pontin's holiday camp, before returning to the station with views of the River Avon. Features of the line included signals, a bridge, a tunnel and a level crossing, whilst the station platform was equipped with a bookstall and buffet.

Operating the line for a number of years was *Coronation Scot*, a stream-lined 4−6−2 steam locomotive based on the famous LMS engines. It was built by Dove of Nottingham in 1946. By the mid-1970s this had been joined by an American type 4−4−0 diesel-powered steam locomotive, built in 1972. The railway was still operating in 1983, but has since closed, and the track has been removed.

Westwards from Christchurch is Tuckton Bridge on the outskirts of Bournemouth. In Stour Road is 'Tucktonia', a 21 acre leisure park. The first miniature railway was opened in 1973. This was a 10¼ in. gauge line circling part of the complex. Nothing is known of the rolling stock used on this first line.

The line closed at the end of the 1980 season, and was rebuilt to 7¼ in. gauge by Narogauge Ltd, reopening on 1st April, 1981. At the same time, the line was extended to approximately ½ mile, running alongside the River Stour.

To operate the new line, new locomotives and rolling stock were obtained, so that by 1985 six locomotives were in stock. Two of these, *Tinkerbell* and *Talos* were 0−4−2 tank locomotives built by Roger Marsh in 1968 and 1981 respectively. Other Marsh locomotives were No. 6 *Medea*, a 2−6−2 well tank, and *Sapper*, a 4−6−0 tank locomotive with tender built in 1982. The other two locomotives were *Sir Goss*, a freelance 2−4−0 tank with tender new in 1982, and *The Bug*, a freelance four-wheeled petrol-mechanical locomotive. Passenger rolling stock at this time consisted of a number of closed bogie coaches built by J. Haylock, plus several sit-astride coaches.

By October 1986 there had been a change of management of the railway, and the line had been taken over by the Tucktonia management. Under them, a new diesel locomotive was introduced. The previous ticket system was also replaced by a token system to avoid cash-handling by the train staff. The railway has since closed.

Joined on to Christchurch is larger neighbour **Bournemouth** which is unusual among the larger holiday towns in not having a well-established miniature railway. There is however a small 10¼ in. gauge line on the cliffs at East Overcliff Drive, not far from Boscombe Pier. The track is in the form of a continuous loop, though no details of rolling stock are known.

A very busy scene on the 10¼ in. gauge line at Weymouth. The motive power is one of the two Curwen-built locomotives used on the line which had closed by 1971.

Oakwood Collection

Weymouth's first Miniature Railway was situated at the Greenhill Amusement Park. Here we see steam-outline diesel locomotive *Auld Reekie* in 1935 with a short train, and apparently displaying a 'Queen of Scots' headboard!

R.W. Kidner

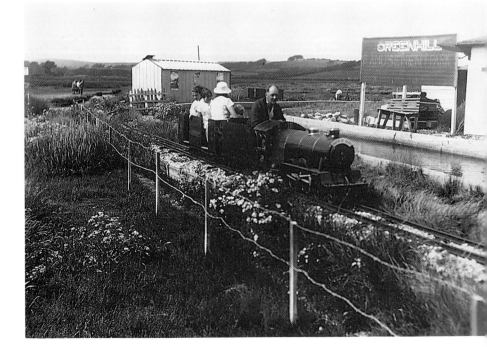

Continuing westwards from Bournemouth, we come to **Poole**.

The 10¼ in. gauge line in Poole Park was once one of a trio of lines operated by Southern Miniature Railways Ltd (SMR) of Southsea, the others being at Southsea and Bognor Regis. The Poole line opened in 1949 and was largely the work of Mr George Vimpany.

The line is approximately ¾ mile long, and encircles the park lake. Unfortunately, because of possible vandalism, buildings and other features are limited to a small station which was built in 1962 at a different point on the circuit so as not to obstruct the view from a nearby restaurant. Mr Vimpany retired in 1979, but fortunately the railway passed to new owners who have continued its operation.

Each of the SMR railways originally had an identical freelance 4−4−2 locomotive built at the company's Southsea workshops. The one used at Poole was numbered 1001, and carried the name Vanguard. This locomotive was withdrawn in 1965 and subsequently scrapped, since which time the line has been operated by petrol-driven locomotives.

Two of the three petrol locomotives in stock today were built at the Poole workshop. These are a freelance Co-Bo locomotive numbered D1007, built in 1959, and a 1963 Bo-Bo numbered D7000. This latter machine is expected to be rebuilt in the form of an InterCity 125 locomotive in due course.

The latest acquisition is a petrol-driven model of Flying Scotsman, though it seems that this will have to run, not as a 4−6−2, but as an 0−6−0 because of the sharp curves encountered on the line!

The five open bogie coaches were all built in the Poole workshop, four in 1949 and one in 1984.

Inland from the centre of Poole is Hamworthy Park which once had a 10¼ in. gauge miniature railway. Very little is known of this system, except that it was in operation in 1971, but had closed by the summer of 1975. The only known item of rolling stock was an unnamed four-wheeled petrol locomotive built by G. Wilcox. It is believed that the entire line was bought by someone from Melton Mowbray for further use.

Our final visit in this chapter is to the port of **Weymouth**, which has had four miniature railways over the years, of which only one is still in operation.

The first line to be built was begun in 1934, and was the work of W.L. Jennings. The railway was built to a gauge of 9½ in. and formed an oval loop 400 yards in length, at the Greenhill Amusement Park on the seafront. Some sources say that it took until 1936 to complete the railway. Two locomotives are known to have worked on the line, though which came first is not known. One was a replica of a Baltimore & Ohio Railroad 4−4−2 locomotive numbered 1430 and named Lake Shore, whilst the other was an internal combustion, steam-outline 4−4−2 named Auld Reekie.

The second line, the Weymouth Miniature Railway, opened in June 1947. It was a 10¼ in. gauge line situated at the western end of Radipole Lake, on the eastern side of the town. The line was approximately 1100 yards in length in the form of a balloon loop with trains departing from and returning to a station located near to Abbotsbury Road. An interesting point about this line is that it was owned and operated by miniature railway engineer David

Curwen and two partners, and it is not therefore surprising that the two steam locomotives used on the line were built by David Curwen. They were No. 2001 *Robin Hood*, a 4−6−2 locomotive, and No. 2005 *Black Prince*, 4−4−2. By 1971 the line was closed, and the locomotives were believed to be in store.

The third line was situated at Bowleaze Cove some two miles from the town centre. The site was a family entertainment centre with children's rides, fishing, swimming and indoor amusement hall. This 7¼ in. gauge railway was opened in May 1975, and consisted of a circular track 150 yards in length, and incorporated a short tunnel. Adjacent to the station platform was a two-road engine shed. Motive power was initially a freelance battery-electric bogie locomotive built by T. Smith of Lechlade, but, by 1977, it was anticipated that a steam locomotive would be in operation, though no details of this are known. Two covered bogie coaches were also constructed by T. Smith. The railway is thought to have closed within the last five years.

The most recent line to be built in the Weymouth area is situated at the Lodmoor Country Park, a couple of miles north-east of the town, on land adjacent to Weymouth Bay. A 10¼ in. gauge line was opened around 1987, and is approximately half a mile in length. No details of rolling stock are known, but the tickets depict a steam locomotive. The line is known as the Weymouth Bay Miniature Railway.

THE MINIATURE RAILWAY, HAYLING ISLAND

A freelance 4−6−2 locomotive at work on the Hayling Island Miniature Railway.
Lens of Sutton

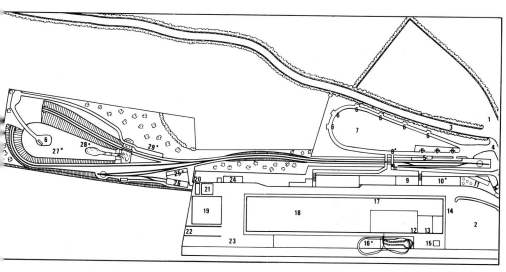

A plan of the Beer Heights Light Railway at Peco's Modelrama Complex.

Steam and diesel on the Beer Heights Light Railway in East Devon. On the left is *Thomas II*, with *Jimmy* on the right as they leave Much Natter station.   *S.C. Pritchard*

Miniature Railways of South-West England

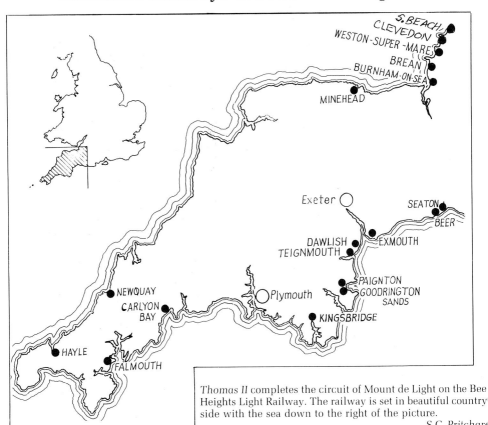

Thomas II completes the circuit of Mount de Light on the Bee Heights Light Railway. The railway is set in beautiful country side with the sea down to the right of the picture.

S.C. Pritchard

Chapter Five
South-West England

CHANNEL ISLANDS – BEER – EXMOUTH – DAWLISH – TEIGNMOUTH –
PAIGNTON – GOODRINGTON – KINGSBRIDGE – CARLYON BAY –
FALMOUTH – HAYLE – NEWQUAY – MINEHEAD – BURNHAM-ON-SEA
– BERROW – BREAN – WESTON-SUPER-MARE – CLEVEDON – SEVERN
BEACH

The port of Weymouth sees regular sailings to the Channel Islands of
Jersey and Guernsey, and it is therefore appropriate at this stage in our
journey around the coastline to leave the mainland, and examine two
miniature railways there.

Jersey at one time had a 7¼ in. gauge line, though its location is not
known. A model of the 'Royal Scot' class locomotive No. 6100 once operated
here, but had been sold to the Little Western Railway at Newquay by 1971.

The island of **Guernsey** has a 7¼ in. gauge line at Sausmarez Manor in St
Martins, which is about one mile west of Fermain Bay on the south-east
corner of the island. The line is believed to be around ¼ mile in length in the
form of a woodland loop. Both steam and diesel locomotives are understood
to be operated, though no further details are known.

Returning to the mainland, and resuming our travels, our next visit is to
the attractive village of **Beer**, once famous for smuggling and lace-making.
High above the village, overlooking Lyme Bay are the premises of Peco, the
well-known manufacturers of model railway equipment. The site is also the
home of the Beer Heights Light Railway.

The 7¼ in. gauge railway was opened on 14th July, 1975 by the Rev.
W. Awdry, author of the famous 'Thomas the Tank Engine' books. As
originally built, the line ran for approximately ⅓ mile from a station at
'Much Natter' to 'Upsan Down', where the locomotive and rolling stock
sheds are situated.

Within a year of opening, plans were drawn up for an extension of the
line, and soon the tracks were extended through Devil's Gorge to a new
station at 'Little Doing'. From here, trains continued back to 'Much Natter'.
Today, a station platform is situated at 'White Falls', opposite the sheds.

A major extension was opened on 1st August, 1982 taking the line through
a 160 ft-long tunnel beneath the car park to Mount de Light, where trains
turned by means of a balloon loop.

The most recent extension was opened on Spring Bank Holiday, 1988, and
takes the line around Wildway Park, a wild tree and grassland area with a
lake. At the far end of this extension is a short platform named 'Deepwater'.
Trains return from here via a second loop around Mount de Light, and back
through the tunnel to 'Much Natter'. A complete circuit of the line now takes
around 8 minutes.

For such a short line, the buildings are well-constructed. 'Much Natter'
station and the signal box situated between the station and 'Upsan Down'
are of miniature size, though the extensive locomotive shed and workshops
are of concrete garage type. A turntable also exists at 'Much Natter', and one
is also situated close to the sheds.

The initial rolling stock consisted of No. 1, a Cromar White four-wheeled battery-electric steeple cab locomotive named *Little Nell* (Works No. E7039), and No. 2 *Thomas Jnr*, an 0–4–0 saddle tank locomotive with tender, built by Richards Engineering. Both were built for the line in 1975.

Since then, three more steam locomotives, plus a diesel locomotive have been added to stock, as follows:

No. 3   *Dickie* is a Curwen 0–4–2 with tender, built in 1977. This is in dark red livery.

No. 4   *Thomas II*, an 0–4–0 with tender was built by Roger Marsh, and is in dark green livery.

No. 5   *Linda* is a replica of the narrow gauge locomotive of that name on the Festiniog Railway, and is also in dark green livery.

The diesel locomotive is No. 6 *Jimmy*. This was built by Severn Lamb in 1986, and was named by comedian Jimmy Cricket. It is in dark blue livery.

On the debit side, the first two locomotives have been disposed of.

Rolling stock originally consisted of five 4-seater open bogie coaches built by Cromar White. Today, there are ten 4-seater coaches, plus a six-car set of sit-astride stock which make up the 'Beer Belle Pullman', the individual coaches being named *Aquila, Aries, Perseus, Hercules, Pegasus* and *Cygnus*.

The Beer Heights Light Railway is miniature railway at its best, and the whole Peco complex provides plenty of interest to the model railway fraternity, plus beautifully laid-out gardens for those less interested in railways.

Moving westwards, past the resorts of Sidmouth and Budleigh Salterton, we come to **Exmouth** at the mouth of the River Exe. Here a 10¼ in. miniature railway has been a feature of the seafront for well over half a century. Indeed, in the 1920s, it was claimed to be the smallest gauge railway in the world carrying passengers. The railway is situated in what is now called 'Fun World' on the Queens Drive Promenade. The line consists of a circuit of track in a field adjacent to a play area. A short tunnel presumably provides accommodation for the stock when the line is not operating. At present, a hut acts as a station on the west side of the circuit, though there are traces of a stone platform at the south-east corner which may once have been the station.

Locomotive stock has changed considerably over the years. The first recorded locomotive was a model of Southern Railway 4–6–0 No. 486, which had been built by F.R. Hutchinson of Surbiton in 1909 to raise funds for the London & South Western Railway's orphanage at Woking. This is believed to have arrived at Exmouth in 1925. Much later, an 0–4–2 named *Marjon* was operated. In 1964 an elegant 4–4–2 freelance locomotive named *Minx* and numbered 2003 was in use. This had vaguely North American characteristics. By 1971 a 4–2–2–4 petrol locomotive built by G.M. Densham in 1959 was providing the motive power. This particular locomotive had come from the North Tawton Miniature Railway in Devon.

Currently, an ugly steam-outline locomotive of grotesque proportions is in use in green, red and black livery. No name, number or works plate appears to be carried.

An American-style locomotive at work on the Exmouth Miniature Railway in 1964.
John H. Meredith

This replica of a British Railways 'Warship' class diesel locomotive was at work on
the Paignton Zoo Miniature Railway in 1961.   *John H. Meredith*

The railway is only small, and each trip consists of three circuits of the track. Three red and yellow open bogie coaches make up the rolling stock.

A little to the east of Exmouth is Sandy Bay where a Countryside Museum has been established. Due to be added to the attractions in 1989 is an 18 in. gauge miniature railway. The locomotive is expected to be the Stirling Single which had been built in 1898 at Regent Street Polytechnic, and which later ran at Fairbourne and Jaywick.

To the west of the River Exe, lie the twin resorts of **Dawlish** and **Teignmouth** both of which have had miniature railways in the past, though none are in existence at the present time.

About 1½ miles to the north of Dawlish is **Dawlish Warren**. In addition to being a good holiday beach, there is also a 500 acre nature reserve. During the 1970s, a 10¼ in. miniature railway was running at Warren Leisure Land. This consisted of an oval of track with a siding leading into a shed. Motive power was provided by a Bo-Bo petrol-electric locomotive built by Hunt of Bristol which had come from Goodrington Sands, near Paignton. This featured American-style bodywork, and at one time was painted white and orange, and seems to have been variously known as 'Santa Fe' or 'Devonian'. Rolling stock consisted of three open coaches. The line appears to have closed by 1980.

Surprisingly, the resort of Torquay does not seem to have had a miniature railway, and so we move on to neighbouring **Paignton** which, although it does not have a miniature railway as one of its seafront attractions, is home to the Zoological Gardens on Totnes Road at the back of the town which has had a miniature railway for around 50 years. The zoo itself opened in 1923, and today is England's third largest zoo.

The first line was laid in 1937 to a gauge of 12 in. Little else is known of this line, except that it was replaced in 1946 by the 10¼ in. gauge line which is still in operation today. The initial railway was operated by a pair of Barnard 4–4–0 petrol-driven steam-outline locomotives based on the Great Western Railway 'Dukedog' class. These were named *Princess Margaret* and *Princess Elizabeth*.

When the line was regauged in 1946, the locomotives moved to Chessington Zoo in Surrey. It is not clear what replaced them on the new line, but by 1961 a pair of Bo-Bo diesels was in use. One, named *Jungle Express* was based on the Western Region's 'Warship' class, and numbered D801, whilst the other was named *The Pride of California*, and had been built by Trevor Guest. This was based on an American Santa Fe design.

The present line is around 800 yards in length in the form of a continuous loop around an ornamental lake. The island in the lake is home to a colony of Lar Gibbons. There is one station at 'Lakeside', and trains operate only during the peak holiday season.

Returning to the seafront at Paignton, the next beach along is at **Goodrington Sands**, once the location of a 10¼ in. gauge miniature railway. This was situated at the Peter Pan Playground, and by 1971 was using a petrol-electric locomotive built by Hunt of Bristol. This was later moved to Dawlish Warren. By 1973, a bogie diesel locomotive numbered 1002, and named *Monon* was in use with an articulated two coach set. The track layout was

Little is known of this railway at Gyllingvase Beach, Falmouth. The locomotive appears to be named *Duchess of Ilkeston*. The main thing is that the passengers seem to be enjoying their ride. *Lens of Sutton*

A mid-1930s view of the 10¼ in. gauge miniature railway at Burnham-on-Sea. Pacific locomotive *Western Queen* stands at Burnham Halt station, overshadowed by the Big Dipper. *Photograph from the Geoff Maslen Collection*

similar to that at Dawlish Warren, being a circle of track with one siding. The whole of the Goodrington area was redeveloped in 1987/1988, and is now known as the Quaywest Beach Resort, and the resort's publicity material makes no mention of a miniature railway.

To the south-west of Torbay is the area known as the South Hams, and our next port of call, **Kingsbridge**. The Kingsbridge Miniature Railway is a 7¼ in. gauge line which began operation in 1969. Located at Square's Quay, the railway runs along three sides of the quayside car park. Although the line is single track throughout, a run-round loop at one end gives a total run of about ½ mile with views of the estuary.

Motive power was initially a steam locomotive in the shape of a Great Western 0–6–0 saddle tank, though this was replaced in 1974 by a Bo-Bo petrol locomotive named *Little Bear*. In 1976, a Cromar White four-wheeled battery electric locomotive (Works No. E7050) was purchased new, and this continues in operation today. Named *Heidi*, and with number 702, the locomotive is painted in a smart red and white livery.

Rolling stock appears to consist of two sit-astride bogie coaches, one in the form of a petrol tanker.

Today, the railway is owned by enthusiast Geoffrey Kitchenside who also operates the Gorse Blossom Miniature Railway Park near Newton Abbot.

We now cross into Cornwall, which despite its popularity with tourists has few miniature railways.

At Crinnis Beach on **Carlyon Bay**, a little over 2 miles east of St Austell is the Cornish Leisureworld & Coliseum. Originally known as the New Cornish Riviera Lido, the complex boasts the usual beach attractions, plus entertainment, a nature trail, naturist beach, and a 10¼ in. gauge miniature railway. The railway was opened in 1974, at which time it was running an Atlantic 4–4–2 in dark red livery with three sit-astride coaches. By 1980 the line was reported to be around 1000 feet in length, though, by 1988, local publicity stated there was around two miles of track, starting from Crinnis Halt and running to the Shorthorn Nature Trail, returning to Crinnis Halt around a balloon loop.

Later motive power included a Dove-built Bo-Bo petrol-mechanical locomotive named *Texas Ranger* and a Hunt Bo-Bo petrol locomotive, the latter having been acquired from the Drayton Manor Miniature Railway. It is thought that the current motive power consists of one steam locomotive and a petrol-electric machine. Rolling stock consists of a number of Cromar White articulated bogie coaches.

Continuing south-westwards, we come to **Falmouth**, which does not seem to have a miniature railway at present. However, in the early 1970s, an unusual 10¼ in. gauge line existed at Swanpool Beach. The railway was electrically operated by a 40 volt supply fed through the running rails, which were laid out in a figure of 8. The locomotive was of diesel outline, and hauled three Pullman-style coaches. Completing the layout were a footbridge, signal box, and locomotive shed. The line appears to have gone by 1980.

A travel guide to the district records that a miniature railway also existed at Gyllyngvase Beach, Falmouth, though no trace of this has been found.

We have now reached the southern-most point of our journey, and so cross the Cornish peninsula to **Hayle** and commence our northward journey. The town of Hayle is situated a short distance up the estuary from the mouth of the River Hayle, and is also served by a canal. It was once a prosperous town providing machinery for the Cornish tin-mining industry. Today, however, it is largely dependent on visitors.

Two miniature railways existed in the town, at Bird Paradise on the south-western outskirts of the town, and at The Towans, on the eastern side of the estuary.

The line at Bird Paradise was a 15 in. gauge line, around 440 yards in length in the form of a continuous circuit, commencing and ending at 'Cockatoo Halt', each journey comprising two circuits of the track. The railway was certainly in operation in 1976, and may well have opened that year as two locomotives were acquired then. First on the scene was *Princess Anne*, a 4–6–2 steam outline diesel electric built by H.N. Barlow in 1953. This was obtained from the Butlin's Holiday Camp at Skegness. The other acquisition was a four-wheeled Lister diesel, believed to date from 1938 which came from the Axe & Lym Valleys Light Railway project. This was subsequently named *Zebedee*. In 1978, an unusual item was added. This was *Tekkel*, soon to be renamed *Chough*, a Dutch-built 0–4–0 well tank and tender built in 1968 by W.V.O. Heiden.

The railway was still in existence in 1982, but appears to have closed since that time.

The area known as The Towans is composed of sand dunes, and is occupied by camping and caravan sites, chalets and hotels. It is also a popular surfing area. The Towans Railway seems to have originated around 1975 using a Carland-built 4–6–0 'Royal Scot'. It was a 10¼ in. gauge line, and it is understood to have been supplied and built by Cromar White. The track was around ¼ mile in length in the shape of a figure 8, and ran close to the beach. By 1976 the line was operated by a Cromar White 'Hymek' Bo-Bo petrol locomotive numbered D7028, whilst the 'Royal Scot' was on display along with another steam locomotive which had been acquired. This was named *Maid Marian*, and bore the number 1070. It was a Bassett-Lowke 4–4–0 Midland Compound believed to date from 1928. It is thought to have originally run on the 241 mm gauge Jhansi Railway in India which was used to help train new recruits to the Indian railway system. It was regauged to 10¼ in. when it was imported into England.

Rolling stock consisted of three open bogie coaches. The railway was still in operation until 1983/1984, but is believed to have closed since then.

Next up the coast comes **Newquay**, probably the best known of the Cornish resorts.

The hilly nature of the town makes it difficult to locate a miniature railway close to the sea, but in Trenance Park at the back of the town, the 7¼ in. gauge 'Little Western Railway' has run for a good number of years. The line is approximately 300 yards long in the form of a continuous loop. The railway is operated by the same management as the Lappa Valley Railway at St Newlyn East, 5 miles away.

③ WESTON MINIATURE RAILWAY
AND PUTTING GREEN

Situated at the southern end of Weston-super-Mare's Marine Parade, the Weston Miniature Railway runs for over half a mile around an excellent eighteen-hole putting course and along the beach lawns overlooking the seafront. At Putters End Station there is a railway souvenir shop and refreshment kiosk, so mum and dad can enjoy a cup of tea while the children ride on the train.

The railway and putting course are open Easter week, weekends until spring bank holiday, then daily until late September.

The Weston Miniature Railway opened on the front at Weston-super-Mare in 1981. Locomotive No. 1 leaves the station at the head of a short train. Notice the goods truck used to provide a seat for the driver. *Bob Bullock*

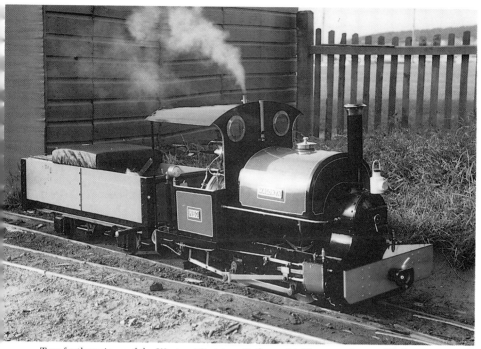

Two further views of the Weston Miniature Railway. *Maldwyn*, an 0–4–0ST simmers outside the engine shed, whilst locomotive No. 1 passes the signal box at Putters Junction.   *Bob Bullock*

In 1971 three locomotives were in use on the line, these being a model of LMS 4−6−0 No. 6100 'Royal Scot', a Great Western 0−4−0 dock tank, and a model of a British Rail Hymek diesel numbered D7002, and built by Cromar White around 1969.

In more recent years, a model of an InterCity 125 High Speed Train has been added to stock, along with an 0−6−0 pannier tank numbered 1366.

Rolling stock consists of a number of unusual open-sided sit-astride bogie coaches.

The next miniature railway was more than 80 miles away on the north coast of Somerset at **Minehead**. Here on the seafront was a 10¼ in. gauge line which was opened in 1965. It was in the form of a continuous circuit, around 400 yards in length. The only locomotive was a Co-Co petrol-driven replica of a 'Western' class diesel locomotive in maroon livery, and named Exmoor Enterprise. Four open carriages completed the rolling stock. Despite the shortness of the line, it was equipped with colour light signals, a tunnel and a level crossing. An unusual feature was that the railway was floodlit during the summer months to allow evening operation until 10.00 pm.

Adjacent to the railway is a model village which contains a 3½ in. gauge model railway featuring a similar 'Western' class locomotive also named Exmoor Enterprise.

Further along the seafront is the Butlin's Holiday Camp, now known as Somerwest World. For many years the camp had a 21 in. gauge miniature railway, though this is no longer in existence. The locomotive used on the line was Princess Elizabeth, a replica of the famous 4−6−2 British Railways locomotive. It had been built by Hudswell Clarke (Works No. D611) in 1938, and had previously served at the Skegness camp. It was in operation here until at least 1971, but, by 1975, the railway had been regauged to become a 2 ft narrow gauge line using an American-built steam-outline diesel locomotive. This has since closed.

The Victorian resort of **Burnham-on-Sea** once had a 10¼ in. gauge line, though little is known of its history. It was certainly in existence in the 1930s, and two locomotives are known to have been in operation. Delivered new to the line in 1934 was a 4−6−2 named Western Queen. This was built by Bullock, and carried the number 1003. It later moved to the Surrey Border & Camberley Railway. Also during the 1930s, a model of a Great Northern Railway 4−2−2 'Single' locomotive was used at Burnham. This had originated on the Pitmaston Moor Green Railway in Birmingham, and is believed to be still in existence on a private line near Stourbridge.

On the northern outskirts of Burnham-on-Sea is **Berrow**, where a 7¼ in. gauge line was opened in 1974. Motive power was a Co-Co petrol-engined model of a 'Western' class diesel locomotive numbered D1017, and bearing the name Western Warrior. This had originated around 1969 on the Forest Railroad at Dobwalls in Cornwall.

About 5 miles north of Burnham is **Brean**. Here, in an area of sand-dunes and caravan sites is situated the Mid-Somerset Leisure Centre. The first miniature line was a 7¼ in. gauge line using an American style 'Union Pacific' locomotive. By 1982, the site had an 18 in. gauge line known as the Brean Central Miniature Railway. The track was 200 yards in length in the

Thirty years separate these views of the Clevedon Miniature Railway. Above is a 1950s view with a Bassett-Lowke 'Atlantic', with more modern motive power below in the shape of a Severn Lamb 'Rio Grande' steam outline diesel.

Bob Bullock and Tom Evans

form of a loop around an entertainments area. A Bo-Bo petrol-mechanical locomotive new in 1975 was in operation with three articulated bogie coaches.

By the mid-1980s a 7¼ in. gauge line existed at the site, but no further details are known.

To the north of Brean, across the estuary is the major resort of **Weston-Super-Mare**, which has had two miniature railways since the last war.

The first was situated on Birnbeck Pier to the north of the town. The pier itself was built in 1867, and is unusual in that the seaward end is on an island. During 1977, the pier gained a miniature railway to add to its attractions. The railway consisted of equipment purchased at the auction of the Axe & Lym Valleys Light Railway in October 1976. Around 300 yards of track were laid, and the line was operated by a Minirail Bo-Bo diesel named *The Cub*, built in 1954, plus two coaches. The line had a very short life, as the pier was put up for auction in September 1977, and the line was dismantled.

The second miniature railway in the resort was established in July 1981 at Beach Lawns, at the southern end of the seafront. This is a 7¼ in. gauge line which runs parallel to the Marine Parade for a distance of about ½ mile in the form of a figure 8. Initially, a steam outline diesel locomotive in pale blue livery and numbered 1 was in use, with three sit-astride bogie coaches. This was later replaced by an American-outline Bo-Bo diesel hydraulic locomotive. There are now three petrol locomotives, in addition to the steam locomotive.

Further up the Severn estuary is the Victorian resort of **Clevedon**. The first miniature railway to be established here is thought to have been in 1952, when a 10¼ in. gauge line was laid on the seafront at Salthouse fields, using a Bassett-Lowke Great Northern Railway 4−4−2 locomotive which is believed to have originated at Cleethorpes. The track layout of this first line is not recorded.

In 1959 a Mr Chivers is understood to have taken over the line, and it seems to have been regauged to 9½ in. By 1971 a Bassett-Lowke 'Atlantic' dating from around 1936 was in use, along with a home-made battery-powered locomotive built by the operator, which was used as a standby locomotive. In 1976 the railway was modernised with the arrival of a Severn Lamb 2−8−0 Wild West style steam-outline locomotive (Works No. 10−5−76).

Our final visit in this chapter takes us to **Severn Beach**, about 8 miles north-west of Bristol. Over the years, this remote location has witnessed a number of miniature railways.

The earliest line was in operation in the summer of 1936, and consisted of around ¼ mile of 10¼ in. gauge track. Motive power was a Bassett-Lowke North Eastern Railway 4−4−2 locomotive which had originated at Hornsea a few years earlier. Rolling stock consisted of three typical Bassett-Lowke open coaches with glass end-screens. Nothing further is known of this line.

During the early 1960s, a 15 in. gauge line was run by Minirail using a selection of diesel locomotives. This operation was relocated to Longleat, reopening in 1965.

Two 10¼ in. gauge lines are also known to have operated at Severn Beach, one known as the Pleasure Gardens Railway, the other as the Lakeland Railway. The Pleasure Gardens Railway is understood to have been run by JSN Amusements, and its locomotive, a Bo-Bo diesel-electric machine built by Hunt of Bristol in 1968 subsequently passed to the Lakeland Railway. This line consisted of a ¼ mile length of track running round the boating lake. Its own locomotive was a 2−4−2 petrol locomotive named *Gloucestershire*. The line ran until being damaged by floods during the winter of 1976/1977, and was subsequently dismantled.

Children on board the Kingsbridge Miniature Railway wave to passengers on the Kingsbridge to Salcombe ferry. Hauling the train is a Cromar White battery-electric locomotive named *Heidi*, new in 1976.   *Author's Collection*

Miniature Railways of Wales

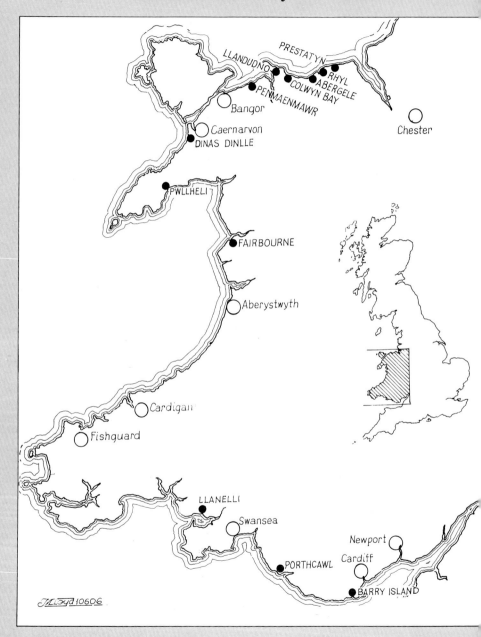

Chapter Six

Wales

BARRY ISLAND – PORTHCAWL – LLANELLI – BURRY PORT –
SAUNDERSFOOT – ABERARTH – FAIRBOURNE – PWLLHELI – DINAS
DINLLE – CAERNARVON – PENMAENMAWR – LLANDUDNO – COLWYN
BAY – ABERGELE – RHYL – PRESTATYN

The Principality of Wales is perhaps more famous for its narrow gauge railways than it is for miniature railways, yet among its dozen or so lines are two outstanding examples at Fairbourne and Rhyl.

Our tour of Welsh miniature railways begins in South Wales at the resort of **Barry Island**, which is popular with residents of the Welsh valleys, and Sundays are particularly busy days. Surprisingly, therefore, there does not seem to be a miniature railway. One did exist many years ago, though little is known about it. A 9½ in. gauge line seems to have been built by W.L. Jennings about 1938, and this is believed to have run around the edge of a boating lake. The only locomotive known to have worked on the line is *Auld Reekie*, a freelance 4–4–2, also built by Jennings. This was based on an LNER 'C6' class locomotive, and was sold to Kerrs Miniature Railway at Arbroath in 1945. It is not known what became of the Barry Island line after the war.

Westwards along the coast is **Porthcawl**, a quiet seaside resort which gained its miniature railway in 1932, when a ¼ mile 15 in. gauge line was laid between Salt Lake and Coney Beach, close to the seafront. It is thought that the line may originally have been single track, but a commercial postcard on sale in the 1970s shows the line as double track with an artificial tunnel covering one track at the midway point of the line. Unfortunately, the line closed at the end of the 1986 season, and has been dismantled.

During its existence the line had only two locomotives, both being petrol-driven, though with steam-outline. The first was built locally for the opening of the line, and was named *Coney Queen*. It must surely be unique in locomotive history in that it was fitted with the controls from an old submarine! However in 1935 it was joined by a second locomotive named *Silver Jubilee*, and in due course, *Coney Queen* was rebuilt to conform with its newer shed-mate.

The rolling stock of the railway was also of interest, as the 12 open bogie coaches were reported to have originated on the Festival Gardens Railway at Battersea.

The next miniature railway on the South Wales coast is situated at the unlikely location of the industrial town of **Llanelli**, on the edge of Carmarthen Bay. Although the town is not a seaside resort as such, it nevertheless deserves inclusion here.

The Borough Council has built a dual-gauge 3½ in. and 5 in. track at Pembrey Country Park which has been developed as a community labour scheme. The line is approximately 1800 feet long, and winds through sand-dunes and woodland, and features a station, signal box and tunnel. The park received the Prince of Wales Award in 1987.

Two contrasting views of Porthcawl and its miniature railway. There are few people about in the top view, yet two trains are in operation. The lower view portrays a more typical bustling seaside scene. The carriage stock began life on the Festival Gardens Railway at Battersea, London. *Author's Collection and D. Gould*

MINIATURE RAILWAY, PORTHCAWL   W 7229

Just across the bay from Llanelli lies **Burry Port**, which, in the mid-1970s, had a 10¼ in. gauge miniature railway at the Shoreline Caravan Holiday Park. The 250 yards-long track was in the form of a continuous loop, and motive power consisted of a Bo-Bo petrol-electric locomotive named *Burlington*, having American-style diesel bodywork.

Across Carmarthen Bay is **Saundersfoot**, a few miles north of Tenby. This is one of two new lines in West Wales, so new in fact that it is not due to open to the public until 1991. The 15 in. gauge line has been authorised by a Light Railway Order and is believed to be just under a mile in length, running from Wisemans Bridge to Stepaside. At the time of writing it was not known what motive power was to be used on the line.

We now head northwards up the west coast of Wales to **Aberarth** just to the north of Aberaeron. Here is the second of the two new lines to be built in West Wales recently. The location is the Aberarth Leisure Park, where a 7¼ in. gauge line opened in May 1990. The track layout is in the form of a circle, but details are not known of the motive power used.

Continuing northwards we come to the small seaside resort of **Fairbourne** where the Fairbourne Railway has had a long and eventful history. Back in 1890, a 2 ft gauge horse tramway was laid by Arthur McDougall who was later to achieve fame with his self-raising flour. The line ran from the Cambrian Railways' line through the village to Penrhyn Point, where a ferry connected with the seaside town of Barmouth across the estuary. The purpose of the tramway was to help in the building of a holiday resort, and although Fairbourne never achieved the status of a popular resort, it is visited by thousands of people who now come to see the railway instead.

As the years passed by, this part of the Cambrian coast began to attract visitors, and so the horse tramway added two passenger cars to its stock.

In 1916 Narrow Gauge Railways Ltd acquired the tramway, and set about rebuilding it into a 15 in. gauge miniature railway. The company already had experience in this, having acquired the Ravenglass & Eskdale Railway the previous year.

In 1922 the operation of the line was taken over by the Barmouth Motor Boat & Ferry Company, and by 1925 was in the hands of the Fairbourne Estate & Development Company. In 1926 an 18 in. gauge locomotive was added to the line's rolling stock, and a third rail was laid as far as Penrhyn Bungalow to allow the engine to operate on the line.

With the outbreak of World War II, the line became neglected and closed in September 1940. During the next five years, the railway suffered badly from the weather, and from the military, and when peace returned in 1945, there seemed little hope of the railway ever reopening.

However, in 1946 three Midlands businessmen formed a new company, Fairbourne Railway Ltd, to reopen the line. The first section, as far as Golf House Halt was reopened in April 1947, and during the refurbishing of the line, the third rail section was removed. Two months later, in June 1947, Penrhyn Point was reached, and the line was completely back in action in April 1948 when the Ferry Terminus was once again reached.

As the popularity of the line increased, a passing loop was installed in 1951, and to cope with the increased traffic petrol locomotives were acquired.

1966   TIME   TABLE   1966

FAIRBOURNE RAILWAY
FAIRBOURNE TO BARMOUTH FERRY - DISTANCE TWO MILES

Calling as required at Bathing Beach, Golf House and Passing Loop.

TIME TABLE No. 1	TIME TABLE No. 2	TIME TABLE No. 3
Daily Service operated From 8th April to 17th April (inclusive) and from 23rd May to 18th June (inclusive)	**Daily Service operated** 19th June to 16th September (inclusive)	**Daily Service operated** 17th September to 1st October (inclusive)

Fairbourne Depart	Barmouth Ferry Depart	Fairbourne Depart	Barmouth Ferry Depart	Fairbourne Depart	Barmouth Ferry Depart
9.30 a.m. E	10.0 a.m. E	9.30 a.m. E	10.0 a.m. E	9.30 a.m. E	10.0 a.m. E
10.30 ,, E	11.0 ,, E	10. 0 ,, ES	10.30 ,, ES	10.30 ,, E	11.0 ,, E
11.30 ,,	12.0 noon	10.30 ,,	11. 0 ,,	11.30 ,,	12.0 noon
12.30 p.m.	1.0 p.m.	11. 0 ,, ES	11.30 ,, ES	12.30 p.m.	1.0 p.m.
1.30 ,,	2.0 ,,	11.30 ,,	12. 0 noon	1.30 ,,	2.0 ,,
2.30 ,,	3.0 ,,	12. 0 noon ES	12.30 p.m. ES	2.30 ,,	3.0 ,,
3.30 ,,	4.0 ,,	12.30 p.m.	1. 0 SO	3.30 ,,	4.0 ,,
4.30 ,,	5.0 ,,	1.30 ,,	1.30 ,, ES	4.30 ,,	5.0 ,,
5.30 ,,	6.0 ,,	2. 0 ,, ES	2. 0 ,,	5.30 ,,	6.0 ,,
—	—	2.30 ,,	2.30 ,, ES	—	—
—	—	3. 0 ,, ES	3. 0 ,,	—	—
—	—	3.30 ,,	3.30 ,, ES	—	—
—	—	4. 0 ,, ES	4. 0 ,,	—	—
—	—	4.30 ,,	4.30 ,, ES	—	—
—	—	5. 0 ,, ES	5. 0 ,,	—	—
—	—	5.30 ,,	5.30 ,, ES	—	—
—	—	6. 0 ,, ES	6. 0 ,,	—	—
—	—	6.30 ,, AES	6.30 ,, ES	—	—
—	—	7. 0 ,, AES	7. 0 ,, AES	—	—
—	—	—	7.30 ,, AES	—	—

E—Except Sundays	E—Except Sundays S—Except Saturdays SO—Saturdays & Sundays only A—Runs during July and August only	E—Except Sundays

Passengers from Barmouth should leave by Ferry at least 10 min. earlier. During inclement weather the service may be restricted or cancelled. A flag flown at Penrhyn Point (opposite Barmouth Ferry) indicates when the train is running.   *Extra Trains will be run as required.

All communications to:—Manager, Fairbourne Railway, Ltd.   *Telephone:* Fairbourne 362

When In Fairbourne Visit The Railway Shop

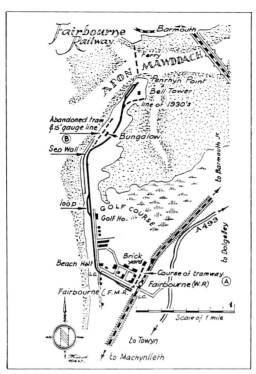

Map showing the Fairbourne Railway.   *Oakwood Press*

Count Louis, a Bassett-Lowke 4−4−2 seen at Fairbourne station around 1930. This locomotive was named after its original owner, Count Louis Zborowski, who was killed in 1925.   *Oakwood Collection*

A rare photograph of Penrhyn Point, Fairbourne in the days before it became a seaside miniature railway. This view, dated c.1900 shows the original two-foot gauge horse tramway run by Mr McDougall. The flag on the right of the picture was hoisted to tell intending passengers that the tramway was operating.   *Courtesy Mr Powell*

A postcard view of the Fairbourne terminus before the railway became commercialised. The locomotive would appear to be *Count Louis* with a full load of passengers.   *R.W. Kidner*

In 1958 a new station was opened in a field adjoining the old terminus which had become cramped. The line then settled down for almost 20 years of continued popularity, but the next few years were to be ones of problems and changing circumstances.

January 1976 began with severe storms which did considerable damage to the line. Good was to come out of this however, for it was decided to extend the line at the same time as the repairs were put in hand, and a 460 yard extension at Penrhyn Point was opened on 22nd May of that year. On 11th November, 1977, the line was badly damaged again by storms which hit the Cambrian coast, and as a result ¾ mile of track had to be relaid at the ferry end of the line.

The year 1980 nearly saw the entire line sold to the Isle of Wight for use on the abortive Medina Valley line.

The railway changed hands in 1984 when it was bought by the Ellerton family who had operated the 12¼ in. gauge Reseau Guerledan line in Brittany. Under this new management, the stations were renamed with Welsh names, Fairbourne becoming Gorsaf Newydd, whilst the station at Golf House was given a totally unpronounceable 66 letter name! New carriage sheds and locomotive sheds were also built at the Gorsaf Newydd terminus. Even bigger changes were to come, for it was decided to rebuild the entire railway to 12¼ in. gauge, and the last 15 in. gauge train ran on 15th September, 1985.

In 70 years of existence as a 15 in. gauge line, the Fairbourne Railway has operated a varied range of locomotives, including the following:

Prince Edward of Wales 4–4–2 Bassett Lowke (Works No. 22)
   Date built: 1915. Driving wheels: 18 in. diameter. Boiler pressure: 125 lb. per sq. inch. Cylinders: $3\frac{9}{16}$ in. × 6 in. Overall length: 14 ft 9 in. Weight: 1¾ tons. This locomotive was sold to the Lakeside Miniature Railway at Southport around 1922/1923.

Count Louis 4–4–2 Bassett Lowke (Works No. 32)
   Date built: 1924. Driving wheels: 20 in. diameter. Boiler pressure: 130 lb. per sq. inch. Cylinders: 4⅛ in. × 6¾ in. Overall length: 16 ft 9 in. Weight: 2¼ tons. This locomotive was built for Count Louis Zborowski's private line at Higham Park, near Canterbury, and was acquired by the Fairbourne Railway following his death in 1925.

Katie 0–4–0T Heywood (Works No. 4)
   Date built: 1896. Driving wheels: 15 in. diameter. Boiler pressure: 160 lb. per sq. inch. Cylinders: 4⅝ in. × 7 in. Overall length: 8 ft 0 in. Weight: 3¼ tons. This locomotive was built for the Eaton Hall Railway of the Duke of Westminster. It later worked on the Ravenglass & Eskdale Railway, and on the Lakeside Miniature Railway at Southport. It was acquired by the Fairbourne Railway in 1922 and was scrapped in 1926.

No. 1 4–2–2 Bagnall (Works No. 1425)
   Date built: 1893. This was a scale model of the famous Stirling 'Single' class locomotive, and had a gauge of 18 in. It was acquired by Fairbourne in 1926, and was sold in 1936 to the Jaywick Sands Miniature Railway at Clacton.

Tracy-Jo, a steam-outlin diesel locomotive based on the Lynton and Barnstaple locomotives photographed whilst on loan to the Fairbourne Railway in 1965.
John Edging

Locomotive *Katie*, a narrow gauge Great Western styled 2−4−2 seen here outside Fairbourne Station in 1966. *John Edgington*

Ernest W. Twining, a 4−6−2 Pacific locomoti built by Guest, at Fairbourne in 1969. It was subsequently rebuilt int an American-style locomotive and renamed *Sidney. John Edgingt*

Ernest W. Twining 4–6–2 Guest (Works No. 10)
> Date built: 1949. This locomotive was subsequently rebuilt into an American style locomotive, named *Sidney* and numbered 362.
> This locomotive was sold to the Littlecote Steam Railway, near Hungerford, when the Fairbourne line was regauged.

Katie 2–4–2 Guest (Works No. 14)
> Date built: 1954.

Sian 2–4–2 Guest (Works No. 18)
> Date built: 1963.
> These two locomotives were a combination of Great Western design and narrow gauge practice.

In later years, petrol locomotives appeared on the Fairbourne Railway, including the following:

> *Whippit Quick*, a Lister 9 h.p. Bo-Bo locomotive new in 1935. Rebuilt as an 0–4–4 in 1956.
> *Gwril*, a 6 h.p. Bo-Bo locomotive built in 1942. This is thought to have been new as a 1ft 11½ in. gauge locomotive. Acquired by the Fairbourne Railway in 1947.
> *Dingo*, a Daimler engined Bo-Bo locomotive, new in 1950/1951.

Work on rebuilding the line from 15 in. to 12¼ in. proceeded quickly, and more than a mile of new track was laid in a matter of a few months. At Porth Penrhyn, a new track layout was installed resulting in the track being closer to the sea. Much of the reconstruction work was done in association with the sea defences, and a new tunnel was built through the sea wall.

The railway reopened to passengers as the 'Fairbourne & Barmouth Steam Railway' on 28th March, 1986 with new and rebuilt rolling stock.

There are currently five steam locomotives in stock, as follows:

No. 1   *Yeo* Curwen 2–6–2T, built 1978 for the Reseau Guerledan line as *Jubilee*. It is a model of a Lynton & Barnstaple Railway locomotive, and is in green livery.

No. 2   *Beddgelert* Curwen 0–6–4ST built 1979 and originally named *David Curwen*. Based on a former North Wales Narrow Gauge Railway locomotive. Maroon livery.

No. 4   *Sherpa* Milner Engineering 0–4–0ST + tender, built 1978 for the Reseau Guerledan line where it was named *France*. It is based on a Darjeeling & Himalayan locomotive, and is in light blue livery.

No. 5   *Russell*. This is a 2–6–4T which was originally built by Milner Engineering in 1979, and previously named *Elaine*. It was rebuilt by the Fairbourne Locomotive Works in 1985, and is in red livery. *Russell* was damaged in an accident some time ago, and was expected to be dismantled at the end of the 1990 season, and parts used in the construction of a new locomotive.

No. 24   *Sandy River*. This is a 2–6–2 replica of an American Sandy River & Rangeley Lakes Railroad locomotive, and was built at Fairbourne, entering service in 1990.

The railway's other locomotives consist of:

No. 3   A petrol-mechanical railcar based on a Rio Grande Southern *Galloping Goose* railcar. This has not yet run at Fairbourne.

No. 6   *Lilian Walter*. This is a rebuild of former Guest & Saunders Bo-Bo petrol-hydraulic locomotive *Sylvia*, new in 1961.

No. 7   *Gwril*, a four-wheeled battery-electric locomotive constructed in the Fairbourne workshops in 1987.

The passenger rolling stock consists of 28 vehicles, some of which came from the Reseau Guerledan line. Many of the carriages are based on Festiniog Railway end-balcony vehicles. An unusual item of passenger stock on a miniature railway is a roll-on, roll-off coach for wheelchairs. Coaching stock livery is red.

The reopening of the line in 1986 proved to be a great success, with a 10% increase in business. On a less happy note, a stationary train was blown over by a gale at a passing loop on 25th August, though fortunately no-one was injured. It is intended that the loop will be relocated at a less isolated spot. The line has also received the Prince of Wales Award for its work in rebuilding the Gorsaf Newydd terminus.

1990 saw the railway celebrate its centenary, and to mark the occasion introduced a replica horse tram hauled by a local horse, the service being marketed as 'Mr McDougall's Horse Tram'. For the future, the railway is working on an extension of the track to enhance further this fascinating line.

Travelling north-west from Fairbourne we cross Cardigan Bay to the Lleyn Peninsula, where the principal resort is **Pwllheli**.

The Butlin's Holiday Camp at Pen-y-Chain, near Pwllheli was unusual in that its railway was a 24 in. gauge miniature railway, unlike most other camps which had narrow gauge lines. It was also different in that the line was used to transport visitors between the camp and the beach, a distance of about 2 miles, whereas the other Butlin's lines were merely just another attraction for the holidaymakers, forming a circuit around part of the camp.

The motive power at Pwllheli was also interesting. The locomotive was a diesel-powered, steam-outline LMS 4-6-2 Pacific named *Princess Margaret Rose*, and bearing the same number as its full-size counterpart, No. 6203.

It had been built in 1938 by Hudswell Clarke, and was initially operated by Butlins on a pleasure line at the Glasgow Exhibition that year. Before reaching Pwllheli some years later, it operated at the camps at Skegness and Clacton.

In the early 1960s, Butlin's began acquiring standard gauge steam locomotives to form static exhibits at their camps, and the one installed at Pwllheli was none other than LMS Pacific 6203 *Princess Margaret Rose*.

Dinas Dinlle on the northern coast of the Lleyn Peninsula, to the south-west of Caernarvon is the unlikely setting for a seaside miniature railway. However, the tourist attractions of Fort Belan included a 7¼ in. gauge line which was opened in June 1978. The site itself consists of a miniature fort and dockyard which were built by Lord Newborough in the 18th century. The dockyard is a replica of the harbour at Antigua in the West Indies.

The miniature railway was in the form of a continuous loop linking the fort with the car park, and ran across sand dunes. The locomotive stock was of particular interest, for replicas of foreign prototypes are rare on miniature railways. The first locomotive to be delivered was *El Meson*, a ¼ size model of a 2 ft gauge Bagnall 0-6-0 of 1913 which was built for the Mexian Eagle Oil Company and operated in that company's livery of dark blue and red. A second locomotive was based on a similar South American Bagnall proto-

Diesel power on the Fairbourne Railway. *Dingo*, a Daimler-engined locomotive at the
Ferry terminus in 1963. The famous Barmouth viaduct can be seen in the background.
John Edgington

Steam at Colwyn Bay. *Prince Charles*, a 10 in. gauge model of an LMS 'Black Five'
class locomotive ran for many years until 1971. By coincidence, genuine full-size
'Black Fives' operated on the North Wales coast line which ran on the embankment
just above the miniature line here. *Lens of Sutton*

The short-lived miniature railway on Llandudno's Great Orme used this model of a New York Central 4-6-4 locomotive which was named *Commodore Vanderbilt*.

Author's Collection

A full load awaits departure of the train on the now closed Prestatyn Miniature Railway. *Reproduced by kind permission of Bamforth & Co. Ltd*

type. Carriage stock consisted of five open bogie coaches, of which four were normally used on a train. The railway has closed in recent years.

Further up the coast is the town of **Caernarvon**. Little is known about a 9½ in. gauge railway which once ran here. Situated on the Slate Quay, it was in existence in 1972, using a 2−4−2 steam locomotive built by Smith of Oldham during the 1930s. It had previously been owned by a Captain Hewitt on the nearby island of Anglesey.

Moving onwards to the North Wales coast proper, we find a number of miniature railways. A line is thought to have once operated on the seafront at **Penmaenmawr**, though no further details are known.

Probably the most popular of the North Wales resorts is **Llandudno**. Since World War II, the resort has had two miniature railways, though there is not one at the present time. The first line to be opened was in 1949. This was a 7¼ in. gauge line situated on what was then known as the 'Council Fields', an area of land close to the town centre, off Conway Road. The site is now occupied by an Asda store. The layout consisted of about 200 yards of single track, and the rolling stock comprised a 4−4−0 locomotive named *Sir Walter Raleigh*, and three 4-wheeled coaches. The entire line was moved to Bridlington, where it reopened in 1951.

The second line must rank as one of the most inaccessible miniature railways, for it was situated on top of the Great Orme, 679 feet above sea level, and reached only by the famous cable-operated Great Orme Tramway. The railway is thought to have opened in 1951, and was of 10¼ in. gauge with around 400 yards of single track situated on a plateau just below the summit buildings. The owner of the line is said to have been the boxer Randolph Turpin, who also had an involvement with the line at Gwyrch Castle near Abergele. The locomotive used on the line was a freelance American-style 4−6−4 built by Dove of Nottingham, and named *Commodore Vanderbilt* and numbered 1951. The tender was lettered 'New York Central'. After the line closed, probably in 1953, the locomotive saw further service at Skegness and at the Peterborough Wildlife Park.

Until 1956, Llandudno was linked to its near neighbour **Colwyn Bay** by the 3 ft 6 in. gauge Llandudno & Colwyn Bay Electric Railway. Colwyn Bay itself has had two 10¼ in. gauge miniature railways, though both have ceased to operate.

The first line to be established appeared after World War II. Originally run by the local council, it was sold to a private operator around 1952. The track was single, about 550 yards in length, situated on the seafront to the east of the pier, and directly below the British Railways main line which ran on an embankment above. The only structure on the line was an engine shed at one end. For many years the railway was steam-hauled using a model of an LMS 'Black Five' class locomotive built by Carland Engineering, and named *Prince Charles*. Its livery was blue with white lining. Rolling stock consisted of five articulated bogie coaches. *Prince Charles* was sold for preservation in 1971, and was replaced by a model of a British Rail 'Hymek' Bo-Bo diesel. Still later, a diesel locomotive with obviously homemade steam-outline bodywork was used. The boiler of this machine appeared to be made out of an old oil-drum! The railway is believed to have closed in 1987 or 1988.

Two early views of the famous Rhyl Miniature Railway. The bottom view shows the impressive station building which was a feature of the line.   *Heyday Publishing*

Just behind the seafront is Eirias Park where a short line was in operation in the early 1970s. Motive power was provided by *Meteor*, a Shepperton-built 2−4−2 diesel.

Approximately midway between Colwyn Bay and Rhyl lies the small resort of **Abergele**. About a mile west of the town, overlooking the coast road from Llandudno to Chester lies Gwrych Castle. Most visitors would be surprised to learn that the 'castle' is in fact a folly, built in 1815 by a wealthy tycoon. However, it does have beautiful grounds, and it was in these grounds that a 10¼ in. gauge miniature railway was established soon after the end of the last war. The track was single, approximately 400 yards in length running on a plateau on the hillside behind the 'castle'.

To operate the railway there was another folly in the shape of a freelance American 4−6−4 locomotive named *President Eisenhower* which had been built by Alfred Dove of Nottingham. This was joined in 1954 by a Bo-Bo diesel locomotive built by the operators, and named *The Chieftain*. *President Eisenhower* was reported to be derelict on the site in 1964. Rolling stock consisted of a six-coach articulated bogie set in red and yellow livery. Also at the site in 1964 was another locomotive built by Dove. This was *Sir Winston Churchill*, a model of the Southern Railway locomotive of the same name, and this could be found on display in a tent close to the railway. The railway was still in operation in 1982 by which time it was known as the 'Magic Dragon Railway', though it is understood to have closed since then.

We now come to **Rhyl** which can proudly boast one of the earliest miniature railways in Britain, and one which has had an interesting history. The town has always been popular with holidaymakers from the Midlands, and even in the early days of this century, the local authority was keen on developing the town for visitors. A large area of land at the western end of the town, close to the seafront had been laid out as a park with an ornamental lake.

In 1910, Miniature Railways of Great Britain Ltd wrote to the Council suggesting that the company should install a miniature railway around the site as an added attraction to visitors. The Council agreed, and in December of that year, Henry Greenly visited the site to survey it. His plan was for a circular track around the lake, which would be laid to a gauge of 15 in. and would be almost a mile in length. There was to be one station at the northern side of the site, with a depot and workshop on the south side. He anticipated one train in operation, running in a clockwise direction.

Construction work began in March 1911, and was completed by the end of April, the opening ceremony taking place on 1st May.

The following year the line changed hands, being acquired by Rhyl Amusements Ltd, who operated the line until it closed for the first time in 1969. The new owners built a loop at the station to house a second train, and an artificial tunnel was built beneath the Big Dipper which was also used to house rolling stock when the line was not in use. In 1920 the locomotive shed was moved to the west of the station. No further changes were made to the line, and for many years the railway held the record for continuous service by a miniature railway.

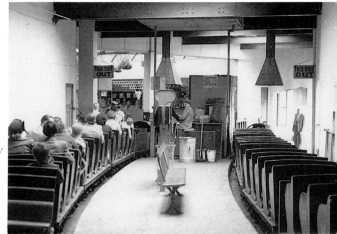

An interior view of the station building on the Rhyl Miniature Railway, 1954. *H.C. Casserley*

An early view of the Rhyl Miniature Railway, with train passing the locomotive shed.
Photograph courtesy I. Gotheridge

Michael hauls a train on the Rhyl Miniature Railway. The locomotive was one of four 'Atlantics' built by Albert Barnes of Rhyl. *John Edgington*

A dispute over the site lease caused the line to close in 1969, and the track was lifted the following year, and the locomotives dispersed, though one was retained by Rhyl Council.

As the years passed by, it seemed as though there was no hope of trains circling the lake again, but then in 1978 plans were announced for the re-opening of the line. New trackwork was laid by light railway engineers Alan Keef Ltd, though it was a little further away from the water's edge than before. A new locomotive shed was built at the eastern corner of the line, and by late summer 1978, trains were running again using two steam locomotives, including one of those used previously on the line.

In 1980, the concession for the line was taken over by Les Hughes, a local fairground, bus and removal operator. Under his tenancy, an American outline diesel locomotive was used on the line. Once again, by 1985, there were problems over the lease, and the line closed down again in September of that year. Fortunately, the track was not lifted, though it seemed that all hopes of the railway running again were dashed when four of the Barnes locomotives (see below) were put up for auction in April 1986.

However, that same year, the railway was taken over by Ken Dove with support from a local Ratepayers Action Group, and the line reopened for a short summer season on 5th July, 1987, using Barnes locomotive No. 101, Joan.

Even now, there is no guarantee that Rhuddlan Borough Council will allow the railway to continue operating, so the story of the Rhyl Miniature Railway is by no means over.

Over the long years of Rhyl Miniature Railway's history there have been few changes to the locomotive stock.

To inaugurate the line in 1911, a Bassett Lowke 4–4–2 named *Red Dragon* was acquired, and renamed *Prince Edward of Wales*. In 1912, a similar locomotive named *George the Fifth* was obtained from the Lakeside Miniature Railway at Southport. Details of these locomotives are as follows:

Prince Edward of Wales 4–4–2 Bassett Lowke (Works No. 15)
   Date built: 1909. Driving wheels: 18 in. diameter. Boiler pressure: 120 lb. per sq. inch. Cylinders: 3⅜ in. × 6 in. Overall length: 14 ft 1½ in. Weight: 1 ton 12 cwt.

   This locomotive originally ran at the Franco-British Exhibition at White City, London in 1909. It was sold to the Dreamland Miniature Railway at Margate in 1920.

George the Fifth 4–4–2 Bassett Lowke (Works No. 18)
   Date built: 1911. Driving wheels: 18 in. diameter. Boiler pressure: 120 lb. per sq. inch. Cylinders: 3⅜ in. × 6 in. Overall length: 14 ft 1½ in. Weight: 1 ton 12 cwt.

   New to the Lakeside Miniature Railway, Southport. Operated at Rhyl 1913–1922. Sold for use at Skegness.

With increasing traffic on the line, the new owners decided to invest in new locomotives. As a result, Henry Greenly designed a locomotive of which a total of six were built by the line's manager Albert Barnes, who was also in business locally as an engineer. Four of the six locomotives, which were based on a North British Railway design, were to operate at Rhyl, the other two being operated elsewhere. The Rhyl locomotives were named after the children of one of the directors of the company. They were as follows:

Joan	Works No. 101	Built: 1920
John	Works No. 103	Built: c1921
Michael	Works No. 105	Built: c1926
Billy	Works No. 106	Built: c1934

Technical details of the locomotives, which were identical, are as follows:

Boiler pressure: 120 lb. per sq. inch. Cylinders: 4¼ in. × 7 in. Overall length: 17 ft 5¼ in.

All four locomotives ran at Rhyl until 1969, when they were stored. *Joan* subsequently worked at Belle Vue in Manchester from 1970 to 1977, and returned to Rhyl in 1984, and has seen some use since. *John* was stored until 1978 when it ran at Alton Towers until 1984, moving to Whorlton Lido in County Durham the following year. *Michael* worked for a short time at Dudley Zoo in 1981/1982. *Billy* was placed on display at the British Rail station in Rhyl in 1986. One of the two remaining Barnes locomotives, *Michael* (Works No. 102 of c1921) has also returned to its home town for storage.

An additional locomotive used at Rhyl was *Clara*. This was in use in 1980, and was a steam outline petrol-mechanical locomotive which had been built by Guest in 1961, and was on loan from the Dudley Zoo Railway.

For a number of years, a short miniature railway existed on land across the road from the more famous line at Marine Lake. This was of 10¼ in. gauge, and its sole item of motive power was a Class '5', 4–6–0 locomotive built by Trevor Guest. The locomotive was neglected at this location, and was returned to its builder before being used on a line at Lowestoft's Claremont Pier.

The final miniature railway in North Wales was situated at **Prestatyn**. Ffrith Beach was the location of the 1600 yards-long 10¼ in. gauge line which ran from the beach to the Royal Lido. In 1971, a Bo-Bo diesel named *Santa Fe* was in operation. This had been built by J. Broome around 1964. Between July 1972 and June 1979, the line was operated by the Ian Allan Organisation using a pair of Bo-Bo diesel-hydraulic locomotives built by Fenlow – No. 10 *Conwy Castle* and No. 11 *Rhuddlan Castle*. The railway had been dismantled by the early 1980s.

A busy scene on the New Brighton Miniature Railway, early this century. A train appears to be entering or leaving the station at the far end of the platform.

Courtesy Heyday Publishing

A scene at the Promenade Road terminus of the Fleetwood Miniature Railway. The Severn Lamb *Rio Grande* locomotive and rolling stock had previously operated at Blackpool Zoo. The Fleetwood line closed in 1982.

Reproduced by kind permission of Bamforth & Co. Ltd

Miniature Railways of North-West England

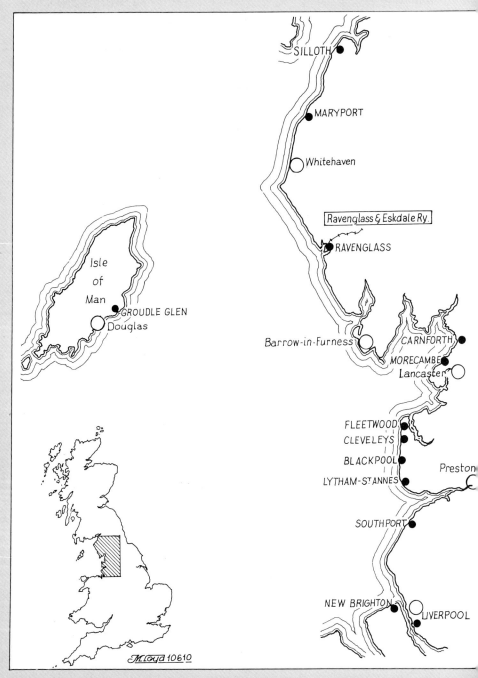

SILLOTH

MARYPORT

Whitehaven

Ravenglass & Eskdale Ry.

RAVENGLASS

Isle
of
Man

GROUDLE GLEN
Douglas

Barrow-in-Furness

CARNFORTH

MORECAMBE
Lancaster

FLEETWOOD
CLEVELEYS
BLACKPOOL
LYTHAM-St-ANNES

Preston

SOUTHPORT

NEW BRIGHTON
LIVERPOOL

M.Loyd 10610

Chapter Seven

North-West England

NEW BRIGHTON – LIVERPOOL – SOUTHPORT – LYTHAM ST ANNES –
BLACKPOOL – CLEVELEYS – FLEETWOOD – MORECAMBE –
CARNFORTH – RAVENGLASS – MARYPORT – SILLOTH – ISLE OF MAN

We commence our tour of North-West England at **New Brighton**. The
Wallasey News for 31st August, 1907 reported that the new miniature
railway in New Brighton run by a Mr Harvey was very popular. The line is
understood to have run from the gates of the Tower Grounds to a quarry, and
claimed to be the smallest railway in the world! Nothing else is recorded
about this early line.

During the late 1930s and early 1940s, two miniature railways are
believed to have operated in the Tower Grounds, though little is known
about them. The second of these lines is thought to have been of 22 in.
gauge, and to have used a Fordson diesel locomotive.

After the war, the Tower Grounds gained its fourth miniature railway, an
18 in. gauge line run by Tommy Mann, which became known variously as
'The Fairy Glen Miniature Railway' or 'Uncle Tommy's Kiddies Railway'.
Tommy Mann was a showman who ran the Marine Lake, and decided to add
a miniature railway to his attractions, and this opened in 1948.

The site was a difficult one, and meant that the railway was restricted to a
length of only 200 yards. The single track line ran parallel to the promenade,
and then turned inland through a sharp cutting, part of which was made into
a tunnel, returning to the station where crossover facilities existed.

Around 1951 a new station was built, complete with platform canopy. A
new locomotive and carriage shed was built, as were a signal box and a
footbridge. Plans to lay a second track around the loop came to nothing. The
railway closed at the end of the 1965 season.

The locomotives used on the railway were certainly out of the ordinary.
To commence operations, Mann acquired a 'Sentinel' locomotive which had
operated on the Jaywick Sands Miniature Railway, near Clacton, in Essex.
To describe this locomotive as a 'Sentinel' is not quite accurate, for it was
built at Jaywick to a Sentinel design. On arrival at New Brighton the locomotive was rebuilt into a steam-outline 0–4–0 tank locomotive, and was
subsequently named *Tim Bobbin*. This distinctive machine was used until
around 1959 when it was scrapped.

In 1951 a Curwen-built freelance 4–4–0 was purchased new, and this was
named *Crompton*, and carried the number '9111-3', which is thought to have
been Tommy Mann's telephone number at the time! After closure of the line,
the locomotive went to Bromyard for use on the Bromyard & Linton Light
Railway.

The third locomotive to be acquired was an ex-War Department Ruston &
Hornsby four-wheeled diesel (Works No. 235624). This subsequently went
to the Ravenglass & Eskdale Railway after closure of the New Brighton line.
They had plans to rebuild it to 15 in. gauge, but instead it was sold to the
Bromyard & Linton Light Railway also. A further move took it to the Bicton
Woodland Railway in Devon where it remains on display.

Rolling stock on Uncle Tommy's railway consisted of the three luxurious bogie coaches which had begun life at Jaywick Sands. They were joined in 1951 by a new coach thought to have been built by Curwen. The three Jaywick coaches eventually moved to the Narrow Gauge Railway Centre at Gloddfa Ganol in North Wales.

The closure of Uncle Tommy's railway was not the end of miniature railways in New Brighton, for, by 1968, a 12 in. gauge line was running in the Victoria Gardens. This line consisted of about 350 yards of track in the form of a loop around the flower beds, passing places with distinctly American Wild West sounding names such as 'Boot Hill', 'Dodge City', 'Blackwater Canyon', and 'Buffalo City'. The motive power did not reflect this American theme however, and consisted of a diesel-electric locomotive named *Golden Arrow*, with a train of three Pullman coaches and two open carriages. The railway had gone by 1971.

Across the River Mersey, the port of **Liverpool** is hardly a seaside resort in the accepted sense of the term, but the city is on the banks of the River Mersey not far from the open sea, and can therefore claim some right to inclusion in our survey of seaside, or perhaps more correctly, coastal miniature railways.

In 1984 the city was the location of Britain's first International Garden Festival, which was held on a 250 acre riverside site near Dingle, to the south of the city centre.

On a site of such size, some means of internal transportation was essential, and it was decided to construct a 15 in. gauge miniature railway to transport visitors around the site. The railway was designed jointly by the Festiniog Railway and Ward Ashcroft & Parkman, and consisted of around 2 miles of track.

The railway was basically worked in two sections. A short branch ran from Herculaneum station at the north-west corner of the site, and joined the main circuit of track at Play Centre station. This line ran parallel to the river for much of its length, and ran through floral displays. This section of line was intended for use by elderly and disabled visitors who could reach the centre of the site without a long walk from the car park. The service was operated by a three-car diesel multiple unit from the Ravenglass & Eskdale Railway.

The main circuit of track could be reached by a short walk from Play Centre station to nearby Festival Hall station. From here, trains proceeded round the site passing the International Theme Gardens before reaching the National Themes section where Dingle station was situated. After this, the line passed close to the Beatles Maze and the Blue Peter Garden. At the north-west corner of the site, a trailing siding led to the locomotive and carriage sheds which were not accessible to the general public. The next halt was at Fulwood station, situated between the Home and Garden Feature and a large lake. Finally, the Mill station was passed *en route* back to Festival Hall station.

Travel on the miniature railway was free, and the service was operated by *River Irt*, an 0−8−2 built by the Ravenglass & Eskdale Railway in 1928, and *Black Prince*, a 4−6−2 from the Romney, Hythe & Dymchurch Railway

Passengers leaving the train at Pleasureland station on Llewelyn's Miniature Railway at Southport. An early Bassett-Lowke locomotive is at the head of the train.
Lens of Sutton

The writer of this picture postcard in 1923 refers to 'this funny little train'. Little did she know of the history of this line at Southport, which still attracts many passengers to this day.
Oakwood Collection

There are few passengers on board this trip on the Southport Miniature Railway. The locomotive appears to be receiving some last minute attention before departure.
Lens of Sutton

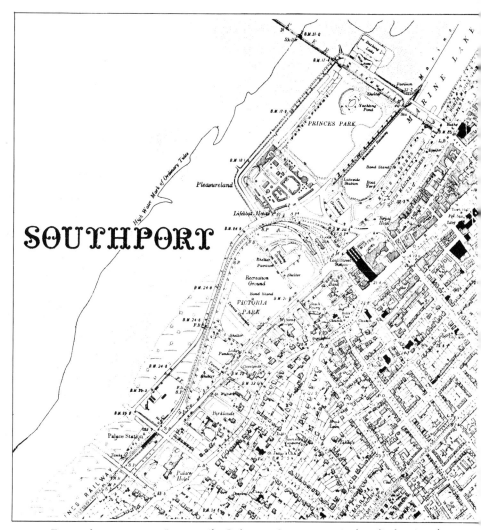

Extract from a 1930s 6″ to 1 mile Ordnance Survey map (*reduced*) showing the Southport Miniature Railway towards the top right hand corner. Also shown is the pier railway, and the standard gauge lines into the now closed Lord Street Station.

Close-up views of three
locomotives on the
Southport Miniature
Railway; *Prince Edward
of Wales, Princess
Elizabeth* and *King
George V*. But for the
lettering, the locomotives
could almost be main line
locomotives, due to the
absence of any rolling
stock or people to give the
game away.
*Lens of Sutton and
Heyday Publishing Co.*

which was built by Krupp in 1937. At certain times, the Ravenglass & Eskdale diesel *Shelagh of Eskdale* was used to enable the steam locomotives to be serviced.

Passenger rolling stock consisted of six enclosed coaches from the Romney, Hythe & Dymchurch Railway, and 21 coaches which were built specially for the line by the Steamtown Railway Museum workshops at Carnforth.

The Festival was open to the public from 2nd May to 14th October, after which the site was handed over to Liverpool City Council for continued use, plus some development. Sadly, the miniature railway was dismantled, leaving the experience of travelling behind steam through beautifully land-scaped surroundings as just a memory.

Twenty miles north of Liverpool is **Southport**, famous for its Lord Street shops, its long pier, and its frequently distant sea. It is also well-known in railway enthusiast circles for its miniature railway, the Lakeside Miniature Railway, which has had a long and interesting history.

This 15 in. gauge line was opened on 25th May, 1911 by Narrow Gauge Railways Ltd. Initially, it was ½ mile in length, running from White City to the Pier, along land leased from the local council.

In 1913, Griffin V. Llewelyn gained control of the railway, and it was renamed 'Llewelyns Miniature Railway', though still retaining the original rolling stock. The Lakeside station was extended in 1919 with two tracks, thus enabling a fuller service to be operated.

During the late 1920s, a local engineer named Harry Barlow became interested in the line, and became responsible for much of the maintenance. At around the same time Southport Corporation became keen to rebuild this line to 20 in. gauge, but nothing came of this scheme. Then, in 1933, Barlow took over the leases on the line, and renamed it the 'Lakeside Miniature Railway' once more.

In 1948 the line was extended at both ends to run from Pleasureland to Peter Pan's Pool, thus making it around ¾ mile in length. The line changed hands in 1969, and with this change came an end to steam traction on the line. The line remains in operation today, and it is well-patronised by holidaymakers.

The locomotives used on the line over the years have been of particular interest. Because the line was initiated by Narrow Gauge Railways Ltd, their rolling stock was in use for many years, being designed by Henry Greenly and built by Bassett-Lowke. First came *George the Fifth*, a 'Class 10' loco-motive, though this only lasted until 1913. In that year, a larger Bassett-Lowke 'Class 20' locomotive arrived, named *Prince of Wales*. Other famous engines to operate at Southport in the early years included *Katie* from Ravenglass, *Mighty Atom* from Sutton Park, and *Prince Edward of Wales* from Fairbourne.

In 1938 a fire at the shed destroyed the two locomotives then in use, *Prince Edward of Wales* and *Sir Albert Stephenson*, of which no details are known. Much of the carriage stock was also destroyed in the blaze. As a result, Harry Barlow built two 4−4−2 locomotives named *Princess Elizabeth* and *King George* respectively.

Ten years later Barlow built *Duke of Edinburgh*, a 4–6–2 diesel-electric locomotive based on the 'A4' streamlined Pacific class. Although the locomotive lacked the subtle styling of the prototype, it was nevertheless a very efficient workhorse, and as a result, Barlow built several others of the same type for use on other miniature lines. There is the possibility that a second locomotive of this type also operated at Southport, for some sources quote an engine named *Prince Charles* as working there.

The next addition to stock came in 1963 when Barlow built *Golden Jubilee, 1911–1961*. This was a steam-outline 4–6–2 diesel electric locomotive very similar in appearance to the gas turbine locomotive GT3 which was then undergoing trials with British Railways. The addition was finished in a bright green livery with a yellow band.

The most recent addition to stock came in 1971 when Severn Lamb supplied a 'Western' class diesel named *Princess Anne*.

In March 1983 a steam weekend was held, for which three steam locomotives were returned to Southport. These comprised *Princess Elizabeth* and *George the Fifth* from Steamtown, and *Synolda* from Ravenglass. Since then the remains of another Bassett-Lowke steam locomotive have been acquired for restoration. So perhaps one day steam traction will return to Lakeside on a regular basis.

Passenger rolling stock consists of 18 open bogie coaches, including a number which originally operated on the Far Tottering & Oyster Creek Railway at the Festival of Britain in Battersea Park, London in 1951.

Also in Southport, the Southport Model Engineering Society operates steam trains on its permanent track, gauge unknown, in Victoria Park on summer Sunday afternoons.

Across the estuary of the River Ribble is the Fylde Peninsula, which has had no fewer than six miniature railways on its 16 mile holiday coastline.

The southernmost resort is **Lytham St Annes** which has a 15 in. gauge miniature railway on land close to St Annes Pier. The history of the line is not known, though the track is in the form of a continuous circuit. Motive power currently consists of a Severn Lamb 'Western' class locomotive and a number of open bogie coaches.

Moving northwards we come to that great British holiday resort, **Blackpool**, which currently has two miniature railways within its boundaries, and also has an important place in miniature railway history.

The South Shore Miniature Railway has the distinction of being the world's first 15 in. gauge miniature railway. It was situated on the sand at the south end of the resort close to where the Pleasure Beach now stands.

At the turn of the century, the South Shore was becoming popular with visitors, and 40 acres of the beach were bought by J.W. Outhwaite and W.G. Bean, with the aim of developing a permanent open-air pleasure ground, similar to those in vogue in the United States. The venture began in 1904, and was an immediate success. At around the same time, Miniature Railways (Great Britain) Ltd was set up by W.J. Bassett-Lowke to build and operate miniature railways, and the decision was taken to establish its first line at Blackpool's South Shore.

A reduced extract from a 1930s 25″ to 1 mile Ordnance Survey showing the Blackpool Pleasure Beach Miniature Railway. Also shown are the 'Scenic Railway', and the tracks of the famous Blackpool trams.

The world's first 15 in. gauge miniature railway was at Blackpool's South Shore, and opened in 1905. Here the Bassett-Lowke 4−4−2 locomotive *Little Giant* approaches the station.   *Photograph courtesy I. Gotheridge*

Blackpool Zoo Miniature Railway's Severn Lamb *Rio Grande* No. 279 at Wells Fargo station.   *Author's Collection*

The booking office and staff of the Blackpool Miniature Railway, 1905. From left to right are the ticket collector, the station master and the guard. Notice the elaborate uniforms.
Courtesy Railway Magazine

A superb 1905 view of the Blackpool Miniature Railway. Sand was to be a problem for the locomotive, and sparks were to cause problems for ladies' hats.
Courtesy Railway Magazine

'Getting up steam outside the engine shed' is the title of this 1905 photograph. For such an early miniature railway, the standards of engineering on this line would put many present day lines to shame.
Courtesy Railway Magazine

The line was a single track irregular circle, 433 yards long, with flat-bottomed rail bolted to steel sleepers, and laid directly onto the sand. The line circled a gipsy encampment with one station, appropriately named 'Gipseyville'. The station itself consisted of an ornate wooden building complete with clock and enamel advertisements. The platform was fenced off, and at the opposite end to the booking office was situated a short siding which contained a single-road engine shed, and an adjacent water tower. The station staff consisted of a ticket collector, station master and guard, all of whom wore uniform.

The railway opened to the public on Whit Monday, 1905, and was an immediate success. It was reported that during the first week of operation 9,600 passengers were carried, many of whom were adults eager to experience this new form of transport. On the busiest day, the train is believed to have run in excess of 30 miles.

The rolling stock consisted of a 4−4−2 locomotive built by the Bassett-Lowke concern, and named *Little Giant*, plus three 12-seater bogie coaches. The locomotive wore a chocolate brown livery, with the letters M.R. on the buffer beam, which many believed stood for 'Midland Railway'. However, the initials stood for 'Miniature Railways', and the six-wheeled tender was thus lettered. The engine was described in the *Railway Magazine* for September 1905 as being the 'most perfect model locomotive ever constructed in this country', and it was felt that although it was basically a freelance locomotive, it bore a resemblance to the North Eastern Railway's '649' class.

Technical details of this early locomotive are as follows:

4−4−2 Bassett Lowke (Works No. 10)
Date built: 1905. Driving wheels: 18 in. diameter. Boiler pressure: 110 lb. per sq. inch. Cylinders: 3¼ in. × 6 in. Overall length: 14 ft 1½ in. Weight: 1 ton 9 cwt.

The line suffered greatly from the effects of sand, which penetrated the axle boxes in particular. Roofs were soon fitted to the carriages, following an incident when sparks from the engine set fire to a lady's hat!

After five years operation, Blackpool Corporation did not offer to extend the concession for the line, and so it closed, and was subsequently transferred to Halifax Zoo, where the locomotive was renamed *Little Elephant*.

The pioneer days of the first 'Pleasure Beach' were coming to an end. The gipsies were moved on by the Corporation, and in February 1910 the original partnership of Outhwaite and Bean became a limited company known as 'The Blackpool Pleasure Beach Ltd'. In subsequent years, the present-day Pleasure Beach was established across the promenade away from the ravages of the sand, and quickly became the biggest and most modern amusement park in the country. Almost 30 years after the pioneer miniature railway began, the new Pleasure Beach was enhanced by a new, larger and more sophisticated miniature railway which is still in operation today.

The second line at the Pleasure Beach was a far more impressive undertaking than its predecessor. Opened in 1934, the line is built to a gauge of 21 in., and is approximately two-thirds of a mile in length. The track layout is in the form of a continuous loop which doubles back on itself at several places and affords an interesting view of the southern part of the Pleasure Beach complex.

There is one main station building which is reached from the ticket office by means of a footbridge. The present station was built in 1970, replacing an earlier 1920s style LMS building. The ticket office and several other features on the line are copied from LMS stations in the Fylde area of Lancashire.

A trip on the line is full of surprises, for in addition to the four tunnels, there is a scale model of the Forth Bridge which once spanned an ornamental lake, but this was filled in some years ago. At various places en route, the passenger is treated to trackside surprises such as prehistoric animals and Red Indians!

The line was initially operated by two Hudswell Clarke locomotives, both built in 1933 especially for the line. Mary Louise (Works No. D578) was a replica of the Flying Scotsman, and appropriately numbered 4472. The other locomotive was Carol Jean, a 4–6–4T (Works No. D579), numbered 4473. Both were painted in green livery, and were named after the daughters of Leonard Thompson, the son-in-law of W.G. Bean, who had by this time become the Managing Director of Blackpool Pleasure Beach Ltd.

Fate dealt a cruel blow to the new line, when on 18th July, 1934 a serious fire at the Pleasure Beach damaged both the Chinese Theatre and the miniature railway. Carol Jean was totally destroyed in the blaze. A replacement locomotive was ordered from Hudswell Clarke, but this materialised not as a replacement 4–6–4T, but as a replica of an LMS 'Princess' class 4–6–2 locomotive in maroon livery. This was named Princess Royal, though sources suggest that it had originally been intended to be named either Carol Jean II, or Geoffrey Thompson, after the son of the Managing Director. It is believed that the name was changed at the last minute following a Royal visit to the Hudswell Clarke factory.

Around the beginning of World War II, the stock of the line was increased by the addition of two locomotives and the rolling stock from the 20 in. gauge Golden Acre Park Miniature Railway at Leeds. The two engines were also built by Hudswell Clarke, Robin Hood being a 4–6–4 tank locomotive (Works No. D570) similar to the destroyed Carol Jean, and May Thompson, an LNER style 4–6–2 (Works No. D582). The rolling stock included a miniature dining car, and a set of wagons also built by Hudswell Clarke. It is not known whether the locomotives were regauged and run at Blackpool, which is doubtful, but they were moved to Morecambe in 1953 to work on a 20 in. gauge line there which was also run by the Blackpool management. Some of the wagons were sent to Morecambe, and the remainder are still at Blackpool, along with the dining car which was regauged and now operates regularly at the rear of one of the trains.

Developments in 1987/1988 have included the introduction of a rebuilt Carol Jean, presumably constructed from spare parts, and the addition of two new coaches. These are enclosed vehicles each seating 12 passengers, and are numbered 11987 and 121087 (presumably their dates of construction). Both are in a maroon livery with white roof.

An unusual feature of the line is its goods stock. Although these are not normally seen in use, they are usually stabled in a siding adjacent to the station, and add an air of authenticity to the railway scene. There are two tank wagons, two bogie flat wagons, two four-wheeled box vans, and six tipping wagons.

There is a standard fare for all passengers on the line, and tickets are standard issue Pleasure Beach ride tickets which are collected by the train driver.

The noise and brashness of the Pleasure Beach may not be to everyone's taste, but it is well worth a visit just to sample the delights of this vintage line.

Situated approximately 1½ miles inland from the famous Blackpool seafront lies the 'World of Animals' Zoological Gardens. The zoo occupies the site of an old airfield close to Stanley Park, and was opened in July 1972 by broadcaster Johnny Morris.

Opened at the same time as the zoo was a 15 in. gauge miniature railway which has become a popular attraction. The line, which is approximately ½ mile in length is laid around the perimeter of the site, and is single track throughout with a midway passing loop. The main station is situated close to the zoo entrance, and the passing loop and terminal stations were initially named 'Toucan Halt' and 'Llama Halt'. However, within months of opening, it was decided to rename the stations in keeping with the American Wild West theme of the rolling stock, and so the stations were renamed 'Wells Fargo' and 'Dodge City', the passing loop halt becoming 'Indian Creek'.

To inaugurate the line, two Severn Lamb 'Rio Grande' 2−8−0 steam-outline locomotives were purchased new. These were painted in an unusual though attractive light blue livery with red coupling rods and cow-catchers. They were not named, but bore numbers 278 (Works No. 7218) and 279 (Works No. 7219), though 279 is also noted as having '7' on the headlight sides.

Enthusiasts and historians seem to have less interest in the technical specifications of internal-combustion locomotives than they do in steam locomotives. However, the following details of the Blackpool Zoo machines are known:

Overall length: 19 ft 8 in. Width: 2 ft 10 in. Weight: 1½ tons. Driving wheels: 12 in. diameter. Powered by a Ford 1600cc petrol engine.

Ten 16-seater toast-rack coaches were also obtained, and these were also painted in blue livery. In 1975 locomotive 278 and five coaches were sold to equip a new line at Fleetwood.

Unlike the miniature railways at some entertainment centres, travel on this line is not included in the price of admission to the zoo, and separate ticket offices are situated at the two terminal stations.

About four miles north of Blackpool lies the resort and residential suburb of **Cleveleys**. Here the entertainments are on a much smaller scale than in neighbouring Blackpool. Jubilee Gardens on North Promenade had a miniature railway for about a decade, though little is known of its history. The line was single track, and trains were hauled by locomotive No. 2,

The huge platform awning dwarfs the 20 in. gauge Blackpool Pleasure Beach Miniature Railway in this 1991 view. The locomotive is Hudswell Clarke 4−6−2 *Princess Royal*.   *Author's Collection*

Locomotive *Robin Hood*, a 4−6−4T steam outline diesel locomotive stands on the edge of the turntable on the 20 in. gauge line at Morecambe Pleasure Park in 1970.
John Edgington

Jubilee, a freelance 4–8–4 steam outline diesel in blue livery, built in 1979. The line is thought to have closed at the end of the 1988 season due to vandalism.

At the northern extremity of the Fylde is the resort-cum-port of **Fleetwood**. The first miniature railway at Fleetwood opened at Easter 1954. This was a 15 in. gauge line linking the Marine Hall Gardens with the boating lake. The railway possessed one locomotive and five open coaches, though no other details are known, nor how long the line existed.

The second railway opened on 19th July, 1975. This mile-long 15 in. gauge line was laid close to the location of the earlier line, commencing at Promenade Road, and running alongside a pitch and putt course, the Marine Boating Lake, and a model yacht pond, terminating at a car park close to the junction of Beach Road and Laidley's Walk. At each end of the line was a shed into which the locomotive worked at the end of a trip before running round its train for the return journey.

The locomotive and rolling stock were not new to the line, having been acquired from the Blackpool Zoo Railway. The locomotive was one of the Severn Lamb 2–8–0 'Rio Grande' class (Works No. 7218) new in 1972, and it was accompanied by five open bogie toast-rack carriages.

Unfortunately, despite an attractive location, the line suffered heavily from vandalism, and was closed and dismantled in 1982. The locomotive and carriage stock were more fortunate, however, being acquired by the Port Erroll Railway in Scotland for further use.

Twelve miles away across the bay from Fleetwood (longer by road) is **Morecambe**, Blackpool's rival for family holidays in north-west England. However, Morecambe is less brash than Blackpool, and has a reputation for catering for older visitors.

The 20 in. gauge line in the Pleasure Park on West End Promenade was opened in April 1953 by Blackpool Pleasure Beach Ltd, the owners of the Blackpool line. The railway was single track throughout with a circular loop at the eastern end, and a turntable at the Promenade Station end. Unfortunately, the line has been dismantled, though short sections of the track could still be seen in parts of the site until quite recently.

The rolling stock consisted of the two former Golden Acre Park locomotives which had been moved from their Leeds home to Blackpool at the outbreak of World War II, and presumably stored until the Morecambe line was built. They were both built by Hudswell Clarke, and were diesel-powered steam-outline locomotives. *Robin Hood* was a 4–6–4 tank engine (Works No. D570), built in 1932, while *May Thompson* (Works No. D582), built the following year was a 4–6–2 identical to the ones in use at Scarborough. Both locomotives were in use at Morecambe until around 1980, since which time the line has closed, and been replaced by a newer line. The site is now marketed as the Frontierland Western Theme Park, and in recent years, a new miniature railway has opened, believed to be on a gauge of 16 in. In keeping with the American theme, the rolling stock consisted of a steam-outline diesel locomotive and western style toast-rack bogie coaches.

At the northern-most end of Morecambe Promenade is Happy Mount Park, where for many years a 10¼ in. gauge miniature railway has existed. The track is in the form of a continuous loop, and there is a tunnel on the back straight which houses the stock when not in use. Motive power is a steam-outline 4–4–0 petrol locomotive numbered 6201, which was originally in use as a steam locomotive.

The town of **Carnforth** lies some 6 miles north-east of Morecambe, and although not strictly a holiday resort as such, it is close to the shores of Morecambe Bay, and thus deserves inclusion here. Carnforth is situated on the West Coast Main Line, and was one of the last steam sheds to be closed in 1968. Soon afterwards, the site was taken over by railway enthusiasts for a museum, and 'Steamtown' was born.

Around 1975/1976 a portable 15 in. gauge miniature railway, around 200 yards long, was laid down on the east side of the site. A passenger-carrying service was operated by Bassett-Lowke 4–4–2 No. 22 *Princess Elizabeth*.

Towards the end of 1977, the railway was moved to the west side of the site. The track was relaid commencing from a platform close to the museum entrance, and was extended by around 150 yards to pass through the main locomotive shed to a small engine shed at the south end of the site, close to the coaling tower. The four-road locomotive shed is of interest as it is entered by means of a traverser to overcome pointwork.

With the help of a Job Creation Project, the line has been further extended to a length of almost a mile, and now ends at a station at 'Crag Bank', which it shares with the standard gauge museum line.

A plan some years ago to extend the miniature line still further would have taken the railway along the shores of the bay to Morecambe Golf Course, some three miles away, but sadly, planning permission was not granted. Fortunately, the museum has a considerable stock of second-hand 15 in. gauge track, so that future extensions of the line may one day be possible.

Several locomotives have worked on the line, including *George the Fifth*, the famous Bassett-Lowke 'Class 10' Atlantic locomotive, and *Royal Anchor*, a diesel locomotive which once operated on the Ravenglass & Eskdale Railway.

In spring 1988 the service was being operated by a 4–6–2 in dark green livery which had been built by Guest in 1946. This locomotive was numbered 5751. In addition, a Bo-Bo diesel in green livery named *Doctor Diesel* was also in use.

Passenger rolling stock consists of a number of coaches built in 1937 for the Dusseldorf Exhibition Park railway, and are similar to those in use at Bressingham Gardens in Norfolk. However, at Carnforth, they have been fitted with roofs. Now painted in a maroon livery, three of the vehicles are numbered 1501–1503.

A relatively recent change has been the renaming of stations on the line. The terminus close to the museum entrance is now 'Northgate Station', whilst the intermediate station adjacent to the engine shed is now 'Westcliff'. The far end of the line remains 'Crag Bank'.

Not far from Crag Bank station, the Lancaster & Morecambe Model Engineering Society have laid out an extensive miniature railway close to the Steamtown line, though museum visitors are not permitted to visit this

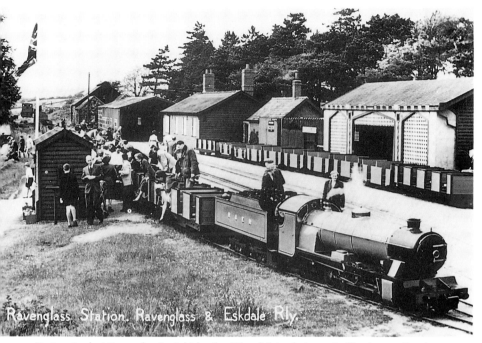

'Just arrived at Ravenglass' might be the title of this photograph. The locomotive is probably *River Esk*.   *Courtesy Heyday Publishing*

A 1930s view of the Ravenglass & Eskdale Railway showing locomotive *River Mite*, an unusual 4−6−0 + 0−6−4 built by the railway in 1927.   *Author's Collection*

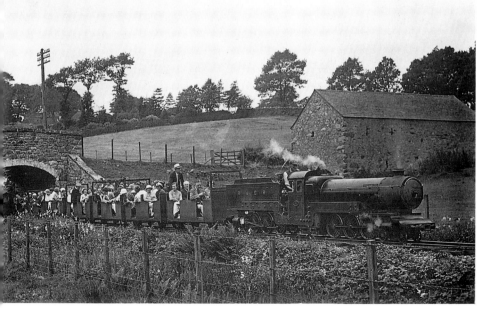

line, which would appear to be of approximately 7¼ in. gauge. A freelance diesel in blue livery, and a pair of maroon bogie coaches are used.

The entrance fee to the Steamtown site allows unlimited rides on both the standard gauge and miniature lines, and no separate tickets are issued.

Although this book is concerned chiefly with miniature railways at the more popular seaside resorts, it is impossible to ignore the **Ravenglass & Eskdale Railway** which has its headquarters close to the meeting point of the Rivers Mite, Esk and Irt on the Cumbrian coast. Originally developed as a port by the Romans, Ravenglass today is a quiet coastal village far away from the more traditional holiday resorts to the south. The railway itself is well documented, but it is necessary here to include a short account of the development of the line.

The Ravenglass & Eskdale Railway had a long and involved history before it even became a miniature railway. The Cumbrian hills around Eskdale were rich in iron ore, and ways of transporting the extracted ore down to the Furness Railway's line at Ravenglass were anxiously sought.

In 1872 a 3 ft narrow gauge railway was decided upon, and this was brought into use in 1875, with a passenger service commencing in November 1876. The 1880s were fraught with financial problems, though the line survived them. Then, in 1908, the Board of Trade announced that because it felt the line was not in a well-maintained state, it would have to close if improvements were not made. As a result, the last passenger train ran in November of that year, though the goods service continued until April 1913.

It was at this stage in the line's history that Minimum Gauge Railways Ltd took an interest in the railway. They took out a three year lease on the line, and a start was made in regauging the track to 15 in. in July 1915. By the end of August, trains were running between Ravenglass and Muncaster Mill, a distance of about a mile. By April the following year, Beckfoot was reached, and the final stretch to Boot was reopened in July 1917.

As the Great War progressed, it became more and more difficult to maintain services, and the service was cut back to Beckfoot in July 1918, but this curtailment was only short-lived. The problem of finding sufficient traffic for the winter months was overcome in 1922 when the Beckfoot Granite Quarry was reopened. To cope with increasing numbers of passengers, the old station at Ravenglass was demolished in 1928, and a new terminus laid out.

An unusual development in 1929 was the laying of standard gauge rails on the section of track between Ravenglass and Murthwaite. This was to enable easier transhipment of stone at Ravenglass, and the new rails were laid on the outer sides of the 15 in. gauge rails on the same sleepers to give a mixed track gauge.

When war broke out again in 1939, passenger services ceased immediately, though the quarry traffic continued as part of the war effort. Despite neglect during the war years, steam locomotives were back in use in 1947.

In 1949 the railway was acquired by the Keswick Granite Company, whose Beckfoot Quarry was doing good business. However, within four years, the quarry was closed, although the company maintained its interest in the railway, and new rolling stock was built, and new locomotives were planned.

The 1957 Finance Act ended the company setting the railway's losses against the profits of the other parts of the business, and the line was put up for sale. There were no buyers for an ailing little railway in remote Cumbria, and in the summer of 1960, the company decided to sell the entire railway at auction, for scrap if need be.

In the nick of time, a preservation society was formed, and the railway was saved. Since 1960 many changes have taken place on the line, including new locomotives and rolling stock, a new station and carriage sheds at Ravenglass, and new track throughout.

In 1976 the railway celebrated its centenary with no fewer than six visiting locomotives from other miniature lines. Additional passing loops were installed at Miteside and Fisherground to allow a more intensive service to be operated. Radio control was introduced in centenary year which will cope with up to five trains in operation at the same time. Eskdale Green Station was renamed 'The Green' in 1979 to avoid confusion with Eskdale further up the line.

No written account of a trip on the Ravenglass & Eskdale Railway can do justice to the beauty of the Cumbrian Fells, so the following description may whet the reader's appetite to visit this beautiful line.

On leaving the station at Ravenglass, the main locomotive and carriage sheds are passed. Soon the line turns eastwards, and the Lakeland hills are spread out in front of the train. The River Mite is now to the left, and once the coastal road passes above on a bridge dating from the railway's narrow gauge days, the first halt at Muncaster Mill is reached, a mile from Ravenglass. Here is a short siding for the use of permanent way trains.

From Muncaster the climb begins, and soon Miteside Halt is reached. The station building here consists of an upturned boat to provide shelter for waiting passengers! Just beyond the 'station' is Miteside Loop which enables Ravenglass-bound trains to pass by. For about two miles, the line runs at the foot of Muncaster Fell, and straight ahead stands Scafell, England's second highest mountain.

Two and three-quarter miles out from Ravenglass, Murthwaite is reached, once the centre of the local quarrying industry, but now little remains of this once-busy place. Just past the former crushing plant is the little-used Murthwaite Farm Halt. Next is Irton Road station (4¼ miles), which remains very much as it was in 1875 when it was the only station on the line with a stone-built booking office.

Half a mile further up the line is 'The Green' station, formerly known as Eskdale Green. The original station building was demolished many years ago, but a new one has been built by the Preservation Society.

This is the steepest part of the journey, and at Fisherground Loop, there is a water column to provide water for the thirsty locomotives. Beyond Hollinghead Curve is Beckfoot Quarry which provided much traffic for the railway for many years. Just beyond the quarry was a request stop for visitors to the Stanley Ghyll House C.H.A. Guest House. Soon the line turns through 90 degrees to the right on the approach to Dalegarth station, and at this point, the long-abandoned line to Boot continued straight ahead.

This rather murky locally-produced postcard depicts on obviously posed view of three Ravenglass & Eskdale locomotives in 1928. The board in the background claims the line to be 'The smallest railway in the world'. The postcard publisher thinks the railway is still narrow gauge! *Oakwood Collection*

An interesting view of Murthwaite on the Ravenglass & Eskdale Railway, taken from the leading coach of a Dalegarth bound train. To the right are the standard gauge sidings serving the stone-crushing plant. *Oakwood Collection*

The present terminus at Dalegarth, 7½ miles from Ravenglass has not always been the end of the line, for the tracks continued on to Gill Force where mining was once carried on, but this branch line closed about a century ago.

Over the years, the Ravenglass & Eskdale Railway has operated a variety of miniature locomotives, including the following which are no longer in existence:

Sans Pareil 4–4–2 Bassett Lowke (Works No. 31)
> Date built: 1913. Driving wheels: 20 in. diameter. Boiler pressure: 120 lb. per sq. inch. Cylinders: 4⅛ in. × 6¾ in. Overall length: 16 ft 9 in. Weight: 2 tons 5 cwt.

> The early history of this locomotive is uncertain, but it is thought to have worked at the Geneva Exhibition of 1913, and the Oslo Exhibition of 1914. At Oslo, it was named *Prins Olaf*. Acquired by Ravenglass in 1915. Scrapped 1926.

Colossus 4–6–2 Bassett Lowke (Works No. 60)
> Date built: 1914. Driving wheels: 20 in. diameter. Boiler pressure: 150 lb. per sq. inch. Cylinders: 4⅛ in. × 6¾ in. Overall length: 18 ft 2 in. Weight: 3 tons.

> Built for Captain J.E.P. Howey's private railway at Staughton Manor where it was named *John Anthony*. Used on the Eaton Hall Railway, 1914–1916. Acquired by Ravenglass in 1916. Dismantled 1927, and parts used in the construction of new locomotive *River Mite*.

Sir Aubrey Brocklebank 4–6–2 Hunt of Bournemouth
> Date built: 1919. Driving wheels: 20 in. diameter. Boiler pressure: 150 lb. per sq. inch. Cylinders: 4⅛ in. × 6¾ in. Overall length: 18 ft 2 in. Weight: 3 tons.

> Dismantled in 1927, and parts used in the construction of new locomotive *River Mite*.

River Mite (I) 4–6–0+0–6–4 Ravenglass & Eskdale Railway
> Date built: 1928. Driving wheels: 20 in. diameter. Boiler pressure: 180 lb. per sq. inch. Cylinders: 4⅛ in. × 6¾ in. Overall length: 22 ft 4 in.

> Built from parts of *Colossus* and *Sir Aubrey Brocklebank* as an articulated locomotive. Dismantled in 1927.

Three narrow gauge style locomotives were also operated:

Ella 0–6–0T Heywood (Works No. 2)
> Date built: 1881. Driving wheels: 13½ in. diameter. Boiler pressure: 160 lb. per sq. inch. Cylinders: 4⅞ in. × 7 in. Overall length: 8 ft 8 in. Weight: 3 tons 15 cwt.

> Built for the Duffield Bank Railway. Acquired by Ravenglass c1916. Dismantled in 1927, and parts used in the construction of an internal combustion locomotive.

Muriel 0–8–0T Heywood (Works No. 3)
> Date built: 1894. Driving wheels: 18 in. diameter. Boiler pressure: 160 lb. per sq. inch. Cylinders: 6¼ in. × 8 in. Overall length: 10 ft 9 in. Weight: 5 tons.

> Built for the Duffield Bank Railway. Acquired by Ravenglass c1916. Dismantled in 1926, and parts used in the construction of new locomotive *River Irt*.

Katie 0–4–0T Heywood (Works No. 4)
Date built: 1896. Driving wheels: 15 in. diameter. Boiler pressure: 160 lb. per sq. inch. Cylinders: 4⅝ in. × 7 in. Overall length: 8 ft 0 in. Weight: 5 tons 5 cwt. Built for the Duke of Westminster's estate railway at Eaton Hall. Acquired by Ravenglass c1916. Sold c1919 to the Lakeside Miniature Railway at Southport.

The current steam locomotive fleet consists of the following:

No. 3   *River Irt* 0–8–2 Ravenglass & Eskdale Railway. Date built: 1928. Driving wheels 17½ in. diameter. Boiler pressure: 165 lb. per sq. inch. Cylinders: 5⅝ in. × 8 in. Overall length: 24 ft 2 in. Weight: 6 tons 5 cwt.

Built from parts of *Muriel*. Current livery: green.

No. 7   *River Esk* 2–8–2 Davey Paxman & Co. Ltd. (Works No. 21104). Date built: 1923. Driving wheels 17½ in. diameter. Boiler pressure: 180 lb. per sq. inch. Cylinders: 5⅞ in. × 8½ in. Overall length: 25 ft 1¼ in. Weight: 6 tons 18 cwt.

Converted to an articulated 2–8–2+0–8–0 in 1927 but rebuilt back to 2–8–2 in 1931. Current livery: black.

No. 9   *River Mite (II)* 2–8–2 Clarkson of York (Works No. 4669). Date built: 1966. Driving wheels 17½ in. diameter. Boiler pressure: 165 lb. per sq. inch. Cylinders: 6 in. × 8½ in. Overall length: 22 ft 6 in. Weight: 6 tons 18 cwt.

Current livery: red.

No. 10   *Northern Rock* 2–6–2 Ravenglass & Eskdale Railway. Date built: 1976. Driving wheels 20 in. diameter. Boiler pressure: 165 lb. per sq. inch. Cylinders: 6½ in. × 8½ in. Weight: approx. 7 tons.

Current livery: muscat yellow.

No. 11   *Bonnie Dundee* 0–4–2WT Kerr Stuart (Works No. 720). Date built: 1901.

New to Dundee Gas Works as a 2 ft gauge locomotive. Withdrawn in 1960, and presented to Ravenglass. Converted to 15 in. gauge with assistance from British Nuclear Fuels Apprentice School, and completed 1982.

Several diesel locomotives have been used on goods trains over the years, though only in recent times have they been used on passenger trains. The first such locomotive was *Royal Anchor*, a 1956 Bo-Bo machine built by Lane of Liphook, which was acquired in 1961. This was sold to the Steamtown Railway Centre in 1977 for use on their miniature railway.

1969 saw the arrival of a diesel-hydraulic locomotive named *Shelagh of Eskdale*, built by Severn Lamb. This was used on the Romney, Hythe & Dymchurch Railway between 1981 and 1983, and was used on the Liverpool Garden Festival Railway in 1984.

A three-car diesel multiple unit named *Silver Jubilee* entered service in 1977, this being another product of the Ravenglass workshops. The latest diesel locomotive is *Lady Wakefield*, a Bo-Bo product of the railway in 1980.

The carriage stock was originally entirely open bogie stock, some of which, dating back to 1928, is still in stock. A number of similar vehicles were built between 1969 and 1972. More recent stock has been enclosed, some with windows (numbers 102–107, 110–117), or others of the semi-open type (numbers 101, 108–109, 118–129). Open bogie stock is painted maroon, whilst the enclosed stock is blue and white with grey roof and ends.

The mid-1980s have seen the railway diversify its interests into the field of locomotive builders for outside concerns. Several such locomotives have

A lightly loaded train on the Ravenglass & Eskdale Railway amid the Cumbrian fells.
Oakwood Collection

A close-up view of *River Esk*, built in 1923. For a time, this locomotive ran as an unusual 2−8−2 + 0−8−0.
Author's Collection

left Ravenglass for private lines, plus a bogie diesel for the Ruislip Lido Railway in Middlesex.

In addition to the operating railway, there is a museum at Ravenglass Station depicting the history and development of the line, and 'T'Laal Ratty', as the line is affectionately known locally seems set to bring pleasure to holidaymakers and enthusiasts alike for many years to come.

The Cumbrian coast north of Ravenglass is not normally associated with holiday centres, but more with industry. However, **Maryport** has a 10¼ in. gauge line, known as the Netherhall Woodland Railway which was originally ½ mile in length, but an extension in 1985 added to this a section containing a new station complete with passing loop. Two locomotives are known to be in use, a Co-Co gas-electric locomotive, and an 0–6–0 gas-mechanical locomotive, both of freelance design.

Further up the coast at **Silloth**, a 7¼ in. gauge line operates on the Lifeboat Car Park. Motive power consists of two steam locomotives plus a petrol-electric machine. One of the steam locomotives is a half-scale model of Ravenglass & Eskdale Railway's locomotive *Northern Rock*.

Our final look at miniature railways of north-west England takes us across to the **Isle of Man**. The only known plan for a miniature railway on the island never reached fruition, though it has of course its excellent narrow gauge railways (including the 2 ft gauge Groudle Glen Railway, reopened in 1986) and tramways. In 1978, a Mr Harrogate of Selby applied to the Port Erin Commissioners for permission to operate a 10¼ in. gauge line preferably along the coast in the resort. The line would have been approximately 400 yards long, but no further information about the line is known.

'Sorry, but you'll have to wait for the next one'. A 1905 view of a train leaving the station on the pioneer Blackpool Miniature Railway.   *Courtesy Railway Magazine*

The west coast of Scotland seemed an unlikely place to find a Cagney locomotive, but here is the Ettrick Bay Miniature Railway in the late 1930s. Note the unusual tunnel in the background. *Courtesy of the K. Taylorson Collection*

The Mull & West Highland Narrow Gauge Railway is in fact a 10¼ in. gauge miniature railway. Here, *Lady of the Isles*, a 2–6–4 tank locomotive stands beside *Glen Audlyn*, the first diesel hydraulic locomotive to be designed and built on a Scottish island. The Isle of Mull ferry is departing in the background. *Courtesy Mull & Highland Narrow Gauge Railway*

Miniature Railways of Scotland

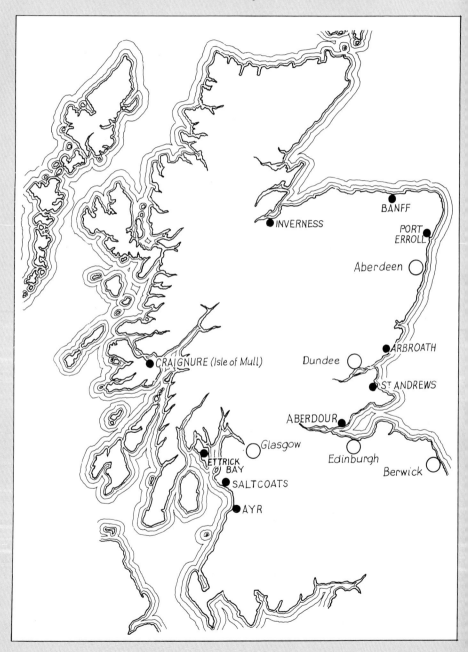

Chapter Eight

Scotland

AYR – SALTCOATS – ETTRICK BAY – CRAIGNURE – INVERNESS –
BANFF – PORT ERROLL – ABROATH – ST ANDREWS – ABERDOUR

Despite the size of Scotland, there are relatively few seaside resorts, and even fewer miniature railways, and amongst those that exist or have existed, several have been located in places well away from the traditional tourist routes.

Continuing our journey up the west coast of Britain, the first Scottish miniature railway is to be found at **Ayr**. Little is known of the 10¼ in. gauge line which has operated on the promenade for over 40 years. It operates only during the summer holiday season, and is in the form of a loop around a children's playground.

Between April and August 1946, a 4–6–2 'Coronation' class locomotive built by Alfred Dove was used on the line before being delivered to its proper home at Skegness. In 1968 a Severn Lamb 'Western' class Co-Co petrol locomotive named *Ayr Princess* was delivered, and this was still in operation in 1980.

About 16 miles north of Ayr lies the small resort of **Saltcoats**. A 12 in. gauge line operated here from the early 1960s until approximately 1980, the location being a plot of open land close to the seafront. Motive power was a 2–4–2 tank locomotive built by Mr Adrian Brough of Watford, and lettered LNER 522. Rolling stock consisted of three sit-astride coaches, built by the same builder as the locomotive.

Our search for Scottish miniature railways now takes us across the Firth of Clyde to **Ettrick Bay**, on the west coast of the Isle of Bute.

Owned by the Rothesay Tramways Company Ltd, this 15 in. gauge line was situated alongside the former tram terminus at Ettrick Bay. The line consisted of a circle of track with an artificial tunnel. As the line opened when the tramway closed in 1936, it has been suggested that tram track was used for the miniature railway. The railway closed with the outbreak of World War II, and was not reopened.

An interesting feature of the line was its locomotive. Named *Samson*, the locomotive was an unusual 4–4–0 built by the McGarigle Machine Co. of Niagara Falls, U.S.A. in 1902. It had originated on the Blakesley Hall Miniature Railway of Mr C.W. Bartholomew, near Towcester. Rolling stock consisted of four 4-wheeled open coaches.

It is ironic that the only offshore passenger-carrying railway in Scotland is a miniature one, and of only recent construction. Situated at **Craignure** on the island of Mull is the Mull & West Highland Narrow Gauge Railway, though despite the title it is a 10¼ in. gauge line, though with definite narrow gauge characteristics.

The railway is operated by the Mull & West Highland Narrow Gauge Railway Company Ltd, which was set up in 1976 to operate a line on the island. Although planning permission for the line was granted in the same year, due to legal and other difficulties it was not until November 1981 that track-laying commenced. Work was completed in spring 1983, and public service commenced on 18th August that year.

The line is just over a mile in length, and runs from near the old stone pier at Craignure Harbour to within a short distance of Torosay Castle. For part of the journey there are spectacular views of both sea and land, before the line turns slightly south to run through a forest to its terminus near the castle, where the engine shed is situated. The track is single except for a passing loop at Tarmstedt.

Steam power consists of a narrow gauge outline 2-6-4 tank locomotive new in 1981, and named *Lady of the Isles*, plus a rebuilt Curwen Atlantic named *Waverley*. Diesel traction includes a replica of a British Rail class '25' diesel which is powered by a Morris Minor petrol engine. During 1986 a new diesel-hydraulic locomotive named *Glen Audlyn* was added to stock. Coaching stock includes a number of enclosed narrow gauge style vehicles.

Our journey continues across Scotland to the east coast, and the highland capital of **Inverness**. Here is a 7¼ in. gauge miniature railway in Bught Park, on the west bank of the River Ness, about a mile to the south of the town centre. The line opened on 31st March, 1984, and uses stock from the former Port Erroll Railway. Two locomotives are in use, No. 1 *Donald*, an 0-6-0 built by Severn Lamb in 1980, and No. 2 *Samson*, a four-wheeled petrol-mechanical locomotive built by Mardyke in the same year. No changes in rolling stock have taken place since the line opened. The track is laid in the form of a continuous loop, and is about ⅓ mile in length.

A short-lived member of the small number of Scottish miniature railways was the West Buchan Railway, a 15 in. gauge line situated at **Banff** on the north-east coast of the Grampian Region.

The West Buchan Railway Company Ltd obtained a 99 year lease on the track-bed of the former Great North of Scotland Railway branch line from Banff Harbour to Tillynaught. The line was owned, in proportions, 80 per cent by the owners of the former Port Erroll Railway, and 20 per cent by the local tourist trade. In addition, the line received a grant of £36,000 from the Scottish Tourist Board.

The line began at the site of the former Banff Harbour station, where it was intended to build a replica of the old station to act as the new terminus. The new track followed the line of the old branch until it reached the site of the former Golf Club House Halt where it turned towards the sea, and ended at a complex housing a caravan site, hotel, leisure centre and outdoor recreation area. The length of the new line was 1¼ miles.

June 1984 saw the opening of the line, and the initial locomotive stock consisted of two second-hand items. First was *Chough*, a Dutch-built narrow gauge style 0-4-0, formerly used on the Paradise Railway at Hayle in Cornwall. Also at Banff was Severn Lamb 'Rio Grande' 2-8-0 steam outline locomotive 278 (Works No. 7218), which had begun life at Blackpool Zoo, before moving to Fleetwood, and finally reached the West Buchan Railway from the Port Erroll Railway.

Unfortunately, the line was not a success, and the company went into liquidation in 1986, with debts of over £60,000. The track was subsequently lifted and the stock sold.

About 20 miles north of Aberdeen lies the village of Cruden Bay, and the neighbouring hamlet of **Port Erroll**. In the early 1980s this was the location of a short-lived 7¼ in. gauge miniature railway known as the Port Erroll Railway.

Standard gauge steam and miniature steam run side by side at Arbroath. Kerr's 7¼ in. gauge miniature railway has been operating since 1935, and in this view an LNER style 4−4−2 is about to depart with a full load.   *Lens of Sutton*

Heading this full train on this trip at Arbroath is *King George VI*, a Great Western style 4−6−2 locomotive. On the left, the 4−4−2 is being pushed round the turntable.
                                                                                    Oakwood Collection

Three locomotives are known to have worked here. No. 1 *Donald* was an 0–6–0 built by Minimum Gauge Railways in 1980, whilst No. 2 *Samson* was a freelance four-wheeled diesel-mechanical locomotive built by Mardyke in 1980. The third locomotive was a Severn Lamb 'Rio Grande' class 2–8–0 steam-outline petrol locomotive which had been built in 1972. When the line closed around 1983, the first two locomotives moved to the Ness Islands Railway at Inverness, whilst the 'Rio Grande' went to the West Buchan Railway at Banff.

Possibly the best-known miniature railway in Scotland is Kerr's Miniature Railway at **Arbroath**. Here in West Links Park, a 400 yards-long 7¼ in. gauge line was opened in 1935 alongside the East Coast Main Line, running from a station at West Links to Burnside. Despite the fact that the town is not a major seaside resort, the line was a great success, so much so that the decision was taken to regauge the line to 10¼ in. in 1938 to allow more powerful locomotives to be used.

The line remained steam-hauled for 25 years, but regular steam haulage gave way to diesel traction in 1960. However, in 1981, steam returned to the line using *Ayrshire Yeomanry*, a 1950 Guest-built LMS 'Black Five' which was on its way to work on the Mull & West Highland Narrow Gauge Railway at Craignure.

Other locomotives known to have worked at Arbroath include *Auld Reekie*, a freelance 4–4–2 based on an LNER 'C6' class locomotive, which had been built in 1938 for the Barry Island Miniature Railway. In later years, this was rebuilt into a petrol-engined locomotive, though still retaining its steam-outline, the engine being mounted in the tender. Also in use was *King George VI*, a 4–6–2 built in the mid-1930s, with distinct Great Western characteristics.

More recently diesel traction has included *Prince Andrew*, a battery-electric locomotive built by the railway in 1961. Twenty years later, a model of a British Rail class '25' diesel locomotive appeared on the line.

The passenger rolling stock originally consisted of six open bogie coaches, though these were augmented by three new vehicles of a similar design in 1981.

In 1978 the operation of the railway was taken over by Matthew Kerr, Junior, and was modernised in 1983, with the building of a new tunnel and signal box.

Southwards we reach **St Andrews**, where Craigtown Park has been the location of two miniature railways. The first, a 7¼ in. gauge line was run by an 0–6–0 petrol locomotive which had come from Aberdour. Sadly, this line was vandalised, and had closed by 1976.

The latest line commenced in 1976 and is of 15 in. gauge, and circles the park lake. The rolling stock consists of a Severn Lamb 'Rio Grande' diesel-powered steam-outline 2–8–0 (Works No. R8 of 1976), plus three coaches, one of which is enclosed. The locomotive, which is unnamed bears the frequently used Severn Lamb number 278, and is in black livery. The locomotive and its train are housed in a shed situated on a branch off the main circuit.

Our final venue in Scotland is at **Aberdour**, a couple of miles west of

Burntisland, on the northern shores of the Firth of Forth, across the water from Edinburgh. Here ran the Silver Sands Miniature Railway, a 7¼ in. gauge line using an 0–6–0 petrol-driven locomotive, which moved northwards to St Andrews around 1975.

Two views of the 12 in. gauge line at Saltcoats. It would be interesting to know who the two ladies were, and why they were being treated as VIPs. *Bob Bullock Collection*

Appendix

Seaside Miniature Railway Tickets

The wide variety of seaside miniature railways, from the lengthy scenic lines to short loops in children's playgrounds is also reflected in the varied ticketing systems employed, and indeed a separate study could be made of these. However, here we have only space to take a broader look at some of the ticket systems used.

Unfortunately for the collector, many miniature railways employ no ticket system whatsoever. This is not confined to the very small systems – many of those included in leisure parks such as the Pleasurewood Hills American Theme Park at Lowestoft offer unlimited train rides in the price of admission to the park, and as no cash is handled by the train crews, no tickets are necessary.

The most commonly used ticket system on miniature railways is probably the use of roll tickets, in which different fare values or classes of travel are met by different coloured tickets. Blackpool Zoo Miniature Railway, the Lakeside Miniature Railway at Southport, and the Exmouth and Poole Park lines are examples of this system. Many different ticket layouts are to be found, ranging from a mere fare (1), to tickets displaying in full the name of the operator and fare (2), or the stations served (3). The Cleethorpes Miniature Railway uses normal roll tickets for single fares (4), whilst the return ones have a perforated section (5) which is torn off on the return journey. Numerous printers produce roll tickets, including Harlands of Hull, Thompson of Sunderland, Henry Booth, Williamson, Lester-press, plus many other local firms.

Automatickets produced by Control Systems Ltd are used by numerous railways. These are issued from machines built into the cash desk counters in the ticket office, and issues tickets of varying colours for different fares or classes (6). Seaside miniature railways using Automatickets include Paignton Zoo, Rhyl Miniature Railway, and the North Bay Railway at Scarborough. The Beer Heights Light Railway uses Automatickets for extra rides not covered by the price of admission to the site.

Punch tickets (7) are a rarity nowadays. At one time, most bus and tram undertakings, plus many other transport operators used this method of ticketing, but mechanised systems have replaced the majority of them. The Fairbourne Railway used Punch tickets for many years, though these have now been replaced by more sophisticated tickets.

The two largest miniature railways in the country, the Ravenglass & Eskdale, and Romney, Hythe & Dymchurch have in the past followed traditional British Railways practice of using Edmondson card tickets (8), the latter having special issues for dogs, bicycles and prams.

Some miniature railways prefer to adopt their own style of printed card tickets, usually produced by local printers. The Weymouth Bay Railway and the Mull & West Highland Railway are examples.

Modern computer technology is now featuring in transport ticketing systems, but only the largest operators can justify or afford such elaborate and expensive systems. The Romney, Hythe & Dymchurch Railway uses such a system, producing attractive tickets (9), giving train time, destination, date and time of last train. The Fairbourne & Barmouth Steam Railway employs a similar system but its tickets are more like supermarket till receipts, only larger.

Few miniature railways are large enough to offer explorer tickets to its passengers, but the Ravenglass & Eskdale Railway makes available an Eskdale Explorer ticket to enable its passengers to make full use of the railway in exploring the beauty of the nearby Cumbrian fells.

Tickets Illustrated

(1) 30p roll ticket – Blackpool Zoo Miniature Railway.

(2) Single fare 20p roll ticket of the Skegness Miniature Railway – the 'ELDC' standing for East Lindsey District Council.

(3) Adult return roll ticket of the Ravenglass & Eskdale Railway.

(4) 25p single roll ticket of the Cleethorpes Miniature Railway.

(5) The detached return portion of a Cleethorpes ticket.

(6) Automaticket issued by the North Bay Railway, Scarborough.

(7) 9d. child punch ticket issued by the Fairbourne Miniature Railway.

(8) Edmondson card ticket issued by the Ravenglass & Eskdale Railway.

(9) Modern computerised ticket produced by the Romney, Hythe & Dymchurch Railway.

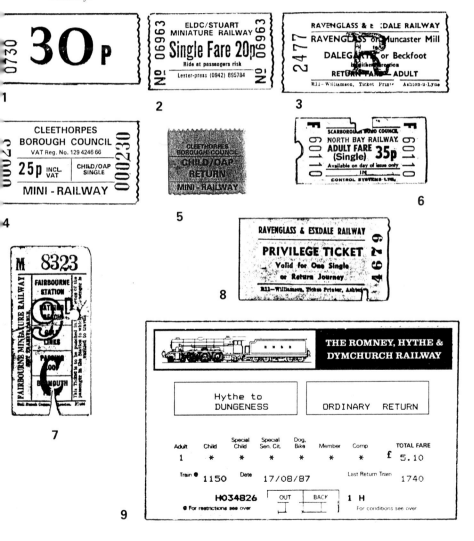

Bibliography

The task of compiling any account of Miniature Railways is made difficult by the lack of printed information. The speed with which some lines disappear often means that nothing is ever recorded, and even those lines which are *in situ* for lengthy periods receive little coverage in the railway press. The following books have proved useful in compiling this present volume:

Butterell, Robin. *Steam on Britain's miniature railways: 7¼ in. to 15 in. gauge.* D. Bradford Barton, 1976.

Clayton, Howard and others. *Miniature railways. Volume I. 15 in. gauge.* Oakwood Press, 1971.

Crombleholme, Roger and Kirtland, Terry. *Steam British Isles.* David & Charles, 1985.

Davies, W.J.K. *The Ravenglass & Eskdale Railway.* David & Charles, 1968, 1981 and 1988 editions.

Davies, W.J.K. *The Romney, Hythe & Dymchurch Railway.* David & Charles, 1975 and 1988 editions.

Household, Humphrey. *Narrow gauge railways: England and the fifteen inch.* Alan Sutton, 1989.

Kidner, R.W. *The Romney, Hythe & Dymchurch Railway.* Oakwood Press, 1967.

Kitchenside, Geoffrey. *A source book of miniature and narrow gauge railways.* Ward Lock, 1981.

Lambert, Anthony J. *Miniature railways past and present.* David & Charles, 1982.

Leithead, R.H. *Stockbook of light railways, miniature railways.* 1971 and 1975 editions.

Morris, O.J. *The world's smallest public railway. (Romney, Hythe & Dymchurch).* Ian Allan, 1946.

Mosley, David and Zeller, Peter van. *Fifteen inch gauge railways: their history, equipment and operation.* David & Charles, 1986.

Scott, Peter (ed.). *Minor railways: a complete list of all standard gauge, narrow gauge, miniature and cliff railways in the British Isles.* Branch Line Society, 2nd. ed., 1990.

Shackleton, J.T. (ed.). *Model and miniature railways.* New English Library, 1976.

Snell, J.R. *One man's railway: J.E.P. Howey and the Romney, Hythe & Dymchurch Railway.* David & Charles, 1983.

Steel, E.A. and Steel, E.H. *The miniature world of Henry Greenly.* Model & Allied Publications Ltd, 1973.

Townsend, Simon. *Uncle Tommy's Kiddies Railway: the story of the Fairy Glen Miniature Railway, New Brighton.* 1986.

Wilson, B.G. *abc Miniature Railways.* Ian Allan, 1961.

Zeller, Peter van. *The Eskdale Railway: a pictorial study of 'La'al Ratty'.* Dalesman, 1985